PRAISE FO

Adam's book is a revel practices that meet chil[...] .... rake nis insights and advice to heart—he has truly captured the essence of playful and meaningful learning. He generously shares ideas and activities for the classroom and, more importantly, for the well-being of each child in schools today and tomorrow. Understanding and using the ideas in this book will help you transform your learning space into a haven of inspired exploration and educational growth. Adam was a student of mine and I am grateful that he has amassed the wisdom found in this book at an early enough age to pass it along to the rest of us.

—Dr. Craig Vivian, professor and chair of the Department of Educational Studies, Monmouth College

This book truly brings back the joy to your classroom. This is exactly what you need to find the engagement your students need and thirst for. So many great ideas to bring the joy of play and FUN—all while your students thrive and learn! A must-read for every early childhood educator!

—Jessica Travis, early childhood specialist and national speaker

All right teachers, get your highlighters and flair pens ready. This book is a must for every educator and jam-packed with innovative and engaging games and ideas to use in your classroom immediately. I found myself having too many ah-ha moments to count. You will find unique ways to mix up what could be seen as boring lessons and gain a new perspective on objects and games you already have in your classroom. I've had the privilege of hearing Adam speak in person. He brings the same passion, joy, and enthusiasm to the pages of this book. Every idea will help you encourage students to master the standards in a way that is exciting and appropriate for children. Find a comfy seat, but get ready to take notes for practical ideas to transform your classroom into a play-based learning environment for your students!

—Hilary Statum, kindergarten teacher and author of the blog *Pencils To Pigtails*

This book is full of strategies for integrating meaningful play into teaching and learning. Adam beautifully shares how to engage learners in ways that promote joy while simultaneously teaching the content standards—and his methods will work with students of any age and require minimal prep time! I plan to use many of his ideas in my classroom!

—Kim Bearden, cofounder and executive director
at the Ron Clark Academy

The natural desire for enjoyment and play should not have to stop when a child enters a school building. Adam not only shows us how play-based learning is practical, necessary, and appropriate for the classroom but proves it does not have to happen at the expense of instructional integrity. By providing excellent examples and stories from his experience as a kindergarten teacher, he makes it easy to see how intentional planning and a little creativity can make your classroom a place where students can learn and play at the same time!

—Adam Dovico, author of *When Kids Lead,*
The Limitless School, and *Inside the Trenches*

Adam Peterson is the perfect person to bring the message of play to our classrooms! He is the real deal! Adam's fun, positive, and high-energy approach to teaching is inspiring. His ideas for play-based learning are not only genius, but absolutely doable! Adam understands that you don't have to spend lots of money or time to create a playful classroom. His strategies are practical and powerful. Learning and teaching have never been more fun. *Teach, Play, Learn!* is a must-have for educators!

—Dr. Lori Elliott, educational consultant and author

When I first met Adam a number of years ago, I thought, *Here is a 6'3" kid!* Adam was filled with excitement and enthusiasm for teaching. When you couple his energy with strategies that engage students in learning, you have a winning combination.

—Deedee Wills, Mrs. Wills Kindergarten

TEACH, PLAY, LEARN!

TEACH, PLAY, LEARN!

How to Create a Purposeful Play-Driven Classroom

ADAM PETERSON

Teach, Play, Learn! How to Create a Purposeful
Play-Driven Classroom
© Adam Peterson 2020

This book is available at special discounts when purchased in quantity for use as premiums, promotions, fundraisers, or educational purposes. For inquiries and details, contact the publisher at books@daveburgessconsulting.com.

Published by Dave Burgess Consulting, Inc.
San Diego, CA
DaveBurgessConsulting.com

Library of Congress Control Number: 2020935495
Paperback ISBN: 978-1-951600-16-7
Ebook ISBN: 978-1-951600-17-4

Cover and interior design by Liz Schreiter

For my father-in-law, Ken,
who would have loved this book

CONTENTS

Foreword..xi

Introduction xv

Chapter 1: Giving Play a Purpose   **1**

  Defining a Play-Based Approach........................... 3

  The Play-Based Approach in Action 5

  Playing with Purpose.................................... 10

  Enter the Doubters...................................... 15

  Next Steps.. 24

Chapter 2: Oldies but Goodies   **25**

  Board Games You Won't Get Bored With 26

  Moving Parts = More Fun! 33

  Deal Me In!... 39

  Thinking Outside the Deck............................... 45

  Final Thoughts 49

Chapter 3: Hands-On Fun!   **53**

  Playing with Food 58

  Standards-Based Play Snacks........................... 60

  Blocks and Cars 63

  Blueprints 73

  Discovery Table... 74

  Sand and Seashells 81

Chapter 4: Play on the Cheap!   **85**

  Next Generation Student Scientists 86

  The Dollar Store Teacher Challenge..................... 97

Conclusion: Just the Beginning   **119**

  Play Beyond the Classroom 120

  Not Just Learning, Wanting to Learn 125

References 129

Acknowledgements..131

About the Author...133

FOREWORD

DR. JEAN FELDMAN

I HAVE RECEIVED COUNTLESS emails from frustrated teachers because they are "not allowed" to have blocks, or dramatic play, or art, or music, or recess—or play! The reality is that all work and no play makes Jack a dull boy—and it makes our children dull as well. After spending months investigating the value of play, I've come up with some insightful information and research that gives credibility to play. Play is not a luxury but is essential to healthy social, emotional, physical, and cognitive development. Classic researchers such as Jean Piaget, Sigmund Freud, and Lev Vygotsky emphasized the importance of play and realized that civilization and the world as we know it could not and would not exist without play. Children have a lifetime to do worksheets and sit in front of a computer. They have only one chance in a lifetime to be a child and play joyfully, spontaneously, and fully.

PLAY! That beautiful little four-letter word at the heart of childhood, sadly, is disappearing. What most adults don't realize is that play is not a frivolous waste of time. Play is the child's work, and play is how young children learn best. The teacher's role, therefore, is to be an advocate for play. The more you know about play, the more you can align it with standards while doing what is best for children.

Friedrich Froebel had the right idea over 150 years ago when he created "children's gardens." Before you can grow anything, you have to work long and hard to prepare the soil. And before children can grow into creative, well-adjusted, happy adults, we have to prepare the soil in their gardens. Singing, dancing, running outside, pretending, building, laughing, exploring—these are the essential ingredients for young children that will create the rich soil from which they will grow the rest of their lives.

As with anything in education, proof is where the power is. So how can we prove that play is beneficial for children? Brain researchers, pediatricians, educators, child psychologists, and theorists all agree that we must protect and preserve play. It is interesting there is no evidence that children who read at five are better readers than those who learn at six or seven. Study after study has shown that children from play-based classes excelled in reading, math, and social and emotional adjustments. They also seemed to fare better in work as adults (Miller and Almon 2009).

When children play, their whole brain is stimulated. Play is multisensory, engaging, creative, and joyful. How many of the senses are actually stimulated when a child plays a computer game?

Play can address many aspects of a child's development. Taking a closer look at each of the four types of development, we can see how important play really is. A child's social development is deeply impacted through play, which helps develop the executive function skills of impulse control, task initiation, and delayed gratification. When children play in groups, they learn to share, communicate, cooperate, and collaborate, all of which are 21st century skills. Without play, we see more behavior problems in the classroom. This manifestation is especially true for boys, because sedentary learning is more difficult for them. Through play, children learn to take the part of different roles and practice life skills that are essential for building relationships with parents, teachers, and friends. Play helps children adjust to school and allows them the opportunity to learn to solve their own problems.

The emotional development of children is strengthened by play as well, as it helps build self-confidence, provides children with the opportunity to master their world, and releases dopamine, which makes children happy. Because play serves as a bridge between fantasy and reality, children tell us things through their play. Play relieves stress and helps children manage their emotions, gives them an opportunity to express new insights and be creative, and nurtures their individual talents and interests. When playing, children learn to experiment and take risks, and they develop self-help skills and independence.

Unstructured outdoor play is obviously beneficial for a child's physical development, but it has also been proven to reduce ADHD and even improve test scores. In children, play develops large and small motor skills, builds healthy bodies, and reduces the risk of obesity.

A child's cognitive skill development also needs play. Through play, children learn to understand the world. Play helps develop language skills and vocabulary. It also lays the groundwork for mathematical thinking and allows children to plan and make decisions.

So, when all of the above is true, why is play disappearing? A multitude of social and cultural reasons exists for why children no longer have the freedom to play. Some of these problems reside with the family, others with schools, from changes in family structure to an increasing emphasis on academics, as well as marketing suggestions that influence the use of educational videos and computer programs over hands-on play. Combine these factors with hurried lifestyles at home and the removal of art, physical education, music, and recess at school, and you'll find that children's lives are sometimes so structured that children don't even know how to entertain themselves. Our new slogan for childhood might need to be BRING BOREDOM BACK.

I'm excited that Adam Peterson has taken on the challenge of writing this book to show you how to turn learning standards into something children want to do instead of something they have to do. You'll feel his joy and enthusiasm as he demonstrates meaningful ways to tie standards to games and hands-on activities. As an educator and parent, he respects the individuality of children and their innate need to play. His heart for nurturing children and helping each child love learning blends perfectly with his teaching skills and extensive knowledge of strategies. Adam will spark your own creativity and rekindle your love of teaching. Enjoy the journey as he shows you that playing makes you smarter.

INTRODUCTION

"**WAIT A MINUTE.** Can you repeat that? *You're* a teacher?"

I provoke that confusion from people quite often, especially from the amazing teachers I had growing up. I don't know that anyone ever expected me to become a teacher, including me. I enjoyed going to school as a child, I loved my teachers, and I usually stayed out of trouble. I admit that I use the word *usually* pretty loosely. If I wasn't engaged, then I would quickly go off task and start goofing around with my friends. Now that I know better, I believe I might have conducted myself as less than an ideal student at times because I needed to be doing things and experiencing the learning.

My favorite subject in elementary school was reading. I was a very creative kid who was always reading, writing, and drawing any chance I got. I would take a notebook and chapter book with me anytime my family was in the car for long periods of time. I would read an entire book on a long drive and then spend the rest of the time writing my own stories based on experiences from our vacation. Stories like *The Wizard of Oz* and *Treasure Island* were some of my favorites because they were full of mystery, action, and adventure. I loved reading The Hardy Boys series as well. I didn't recognize it then, but I think I related to those books so well because the characters were kids, like me, who were learning through doing, just like I enjoyed. I was engaged in reading and writing because I wanted to be, and I learned from it in a way that excited me.

My love of reading adventure stories naturally paved the way for my love of watching adventure movies. Movies were the perfect way to fuel my playful imagination, and they offered me an outlet to another world when I was bored. My dad, brother, and I were huge fans of the Indiana Jones movie series, and I watched *Indiana Jones and the Temple of Doom* religiously. I *was* Indiana Jones in my imagination in any way possible, even at school. Nothing kept my attention inside the classroom more than the playground equipment I could see through the window. I was obsessed with playing on the jungle gym and slides because they were no longer just playground equipment to me. They were temples, mountains, rock walls, and means of escape from the villains from every Indiana Jones movie I had watched.

Though I had some fantastic teachers who cared for me and taught me the basics and other teachers who taught extraordinary units that brought learning to life for me, the sitting and getting style of learning was no match for my imagination and playful mindset. Indiana Jones remained my teachers' greatest competition until sixth grade, when my dad came home one evening with a rented VHS tape of *Top Gun*. I immediately threw out all plans I had for my future; I was going to be a fighter pilot. Even more, I truly believed I was going to be Maverick, Tom Cruise's character. I borrowed a tube of Brylcreem from my grandpa's bathroom cupboard and started slicking my hair over, wore aviator sunglasses anytime I could get my hands on a pair, and wanted nothing more in life than my own bomber jacket. (Spoiler alert: I never got one.) This was dramatic play at its finest. I, a rambunctious little boy, was playing dress-up. My persona took dramatic play to new heights when I zip-tied water guns to the handlebars of my bike, pretending it was Maverick's famous F-14 Tomcat. My brother and I had some pretty intense dog-fights through the neighborhood streets.

I eventually grew out of the movie-hero phase and thought for a while that I wanted to be a musician, race car driver, professional athlete, or firefighter. Do you notice a trend? Every career involved some type of action, play, or excitement. It wasn't until my junior year of high school that I decided to become an educator. The summers surrounding that year changed my life in ways I had never imagined, and I chose my career without realizing it. I spent those summers as a counselor at an Easterseals camp called Camp Independence. I was with some of my best friends enjoying time in the wilderness and having the time of our lives with a bunch of amazing kids. We were given the opportunity to be mentors and counselors for children with varying disabilities, from mild cases of ADHD to severe cerebral palsy.

The best part of all was that I got to be a kid all over again. Though there were adaptations in place for the kids we were mentoring, I was able to relive my own childhood through playful, engaging learning experiences. As a teenager used to the everyday routine of sitting in desks and learning from textbooks, I embraced this new learning opportunity with one hundred percent commitment to not only teach the children I was working with but also learn as much as I could while there. It was no doubt an awesome and challenging experience, but it was also the most inspiring time of my life at that point. When I reflect on the experiences of that summer and the opportunity I was given to witness true learning through play, it makes complete sense that I decided to pursue a career involving children in some aspect of education.

Continuing along this path, two years later I headed off to Monmouth College in Monmouth, Illinois, expecting to enter into a special education program. Unfortunately, the college dropped the program my freshman year because of low enrollment, meaning I had to either transfer to a different college or change my major. I decided very easily on the latter for a couple of reasons. The first was that I had already spent a semester as a teacher's aide in a kindergarten classroom and had loved it. I still had a desire for special education work, but the time I spent in that classroom showed me I had a true passion for the kindergarten level. The second reason I decided to stay was that I had just met my future wife and wasn't about to transfer schools. Honestly, she was the first reason why.

My beautiful wife, Trisha, was also an education major, and together we spent the next three and a half years experiencing college life and preparing for our careers. In fact, Trisha deserves much of the credit for where I am today. If it weren't for her believing in me and pushing me to do better, I wouldn't have ended up here. I wasn't the most dedicated student when I first arrived on campus in the fall of 2000. My freshman year was an eye-opening experience, to say the least.

I grew up in a very small town and never risked getting myself into too much trouble doing anything my parents could find out about. My dad was a volunteer firefighter, and he and my mom both worked for our local ambulance service. This meant that we had a police scanner on at our house at all times. But away at Monmouth, with nobody monitoring my everyday actions, I let myself fall into the mindset of doing whatever I wanted in my newfound freedom. The required general education classes offered little to no opportunity for learning through doing. Even my science classes were nothing more than lectures. I stopped going to class and instead spent my time doing things that better held my interest.

Then, in February, I met Trisha. To spend more time with her, I suddenly wanted to attend my classes. As we entered the courses for education majors, my philosophy was fueled by an entire department of professors who allowed us to learn by doing. I'll never forget Melinda Grimm teaching us children's literature by telling stories dressed up as characters, or Dr. Craig Vivian allowing us to learn by discussing situations we encountered in classrooms where we volunteered. My attendance and grades improved dramatically under the influence of Trisha and my professors. Before I knew it, senior year was upon me, and I began the next chapter of my journey to becoming a teacher—student teaching.

I remember student teaching as one of the best learning experiences I had as a teacher in training. Finally! No more textbooks or lectures. No more days with multiple assignments due. No more classes here and there across campus. I got to spend every day in a classroom surrounded by students, doing what I love to do. I also remember my student teaching as a time of personal transformation, a time when I had to grow from a young, naive, partying college student into a mature, hardworking professional—overnight. That was hard! Especially the mature part.

As much as the world was forcing me to grow up, I wasn't ready. I was excited about student teaching and beginning my career, but it was difficult for me to accept that I could no longer wear T-shirts and jeans every day. Dress shirts, khakis, and ties were taking over my dorm room closet while my Blink-182 T-shirts and baggy pants were pushed aside, only to see the light of day on the weekends. I had no choice but to accept this outer wardrobe change, but my inner self was still very much in the never-grow-up phase. Enter Chris Peterson, my mom. She and I had our share of arguments about my professionalism, or lack thereof, but we had our biggest fight just before student teaching started. Despite the clothing changes I had already given in to, she also insisted I get a haircut. I was a twenty-one-year-old guy being forced to get a haircut by his mother. I wasn't happy at all.

But soon I was in the middle of student teaching and loving every minute of it. I was having the time of my life with Mrs. Vickroy, the best cooperating teacher I could have hoped for. She was a phenomenal kindergarten teacher. She had a knack for making learning fun, no matter the content, and I am forever grateful I had her to learn from. I also had an amazing teaching assistant, Mrs. McCurry, who might as well have been another full-fledged teacher in the room. They both were lifesavers for me, constantly encouraging me, supporting me, and eventually confirming that the way I believed children should learn truly works. Last, but not least, I had a great group of kiddos that reminded me how awesome it was to be five years old.

For the most part, this situation was perfect. I loved what I was doing, with one exception: I was teaching what I was required to teach according to the curriculum, but I wasn't teaching it the way I wanted. Regardless of Mrs. Vickroy's inspiration, I was still bound by a set of expectations from the college. Those expectations, coupled with my inexperience, led to me teach in a style I didn't enjoy, letting the scripted curriculum take precedence over my creativity.

One weekend, I was visiting home. My mom and I were chatting about student teaching, and in the middle of our discussion she gave me a gift. It was a T-shirt! The same lady who was behind my T-shirts losing their place of prominence in my closet had bought me another one. But this was no Blink-182 shirt. Nor did it have any rad designs or bright colors. It was a plain white T-shirt with two short sentences set on its front in a fun Comic Sans font. It read GROWING OLD IS MANDATORY. GROWING UP IS OPTIONAL.

Little did my mom, or even I, know just how much those words would impact me as a teacher. My mom isn't a classroom teacher, but she taught me more than she knew with that T-shirt. To someone else, it might have been a joke about maturity. But I took it more figuratively and immediately started thinking about my own childhood and education. Would my five-year-old self be happy learning from the way I was teaching? Did my own growing up make me forget the learning experiences I cherished most? I immediately knew that the older me needed to remember how much fun school could be. That shirt was more than a gift; it was an affirmation of a fundamental belief I hold for teaching, summed up in one simple phrase: "It's not about *what* you teach but *how* you teach that makes all the difference."

I took that belief with me back to student teaching and started creating my own lessons that broke the boundaries of what the teacher's manual was guiding me to do. I started thinking like a teacher rather than just teaching. It was that year, in the spring of 2004, that I did my first room transformation and play-based unit. In our reading series, we were in the middle of a unit that included a book on the rain forest. My students loved that book and were constantly asking questions about the plants and animals in it, so I decided to take their interest in this unit and run with it. I consulted Mrs. Vickroy with an idea to help their love of the rain forest come to life, and she went along with it! I got busy cutting paper strips, looking for craft ideas on rain forest animals, and raiding the library for every book that had anything to do with rain forests. Within a week, we had turned our classroom into a rain forest, complete with paper-chain vines and student-made animals. It was a remarkable sight to anyone that walked by our classroom, and I was proud of the compliments my students and I received on the way it looked.

The classroom transformation alone would have been enough for me, but to my surprise, it didn't compare to my happiness with the learning experience it sparked in my students. Their desire to learn independently was unbelievable. Soon, *they* were checking out rain forest books from the library; *they* were drawing, coloring, and labeling rain forest creatures; and *they* were pretending to be rain forest explorers on the playground. Success! That transformation—in the room and the kids—was the result of a simple twist on something we were already learning about, but the engagement and excitement it caused with the students and staff at Hedding Elementary School showed me that I was finally becoming the teacher I wanted to be. (Thanks again for the T-shirt, Mom.)

Mrs. Vickroy's leadership and mentorship helped me to be certain that I had found my calling, and I take great pride today in shouting from the rooftops, "I AM A KINDERGARTEN TEACHER!" Looking back now, I spent most of my education career in the best job in the world. I called Room 106 at Saratoga Elementary School home for thirteen years, and it's the place that I was able to develop and practice all the strategies you'll read about in this book. Of course, there was a lot of trial and error. Things did fail. Thankfully, I was lucky enough to work under administrators who believed in my abilities and trusted me to teach the standards in my own purposeful and play-based ways. They realized the importance of our students wanting to learn and supported the use of board games, toys, blocks, and other tools for teaching. Yes, my position had its challenges, its ups and downs. It wasn't perfect, but it was the perfect place for me. Saratoga Elementary is a wonderful school, and I'm a better teacher for having worked there.

After thirteen years in that classroom, I decided to take on a new challenge. I now work as an education consultant with teachers all over the country, sharing my passion for the things I was able to do in my own kindergarten classroom. I love visiting schools and seeing classrooms in action but, more importantly, I love helping teachers plan and implement a play-driven learning environment in their classrooms because I know firsthand the effect it will have on their students. When I spend a day with educators, I allow them to take on the role of students and learn together through games and activities, just like the children in their classrooms will be doing. Part of this process is to help teachers realize how easy it can be to add play-based activities to the curriculums they're already using.

During my time in my own classroom, I had plenty of experience with applying this strategy because I went through many curriculum changes in all the subject areas. We teachers were constantly given new reading series, math series, and writing curriculums. Combine these changes with the modifications and additions to standards over the years, and I was constantly looking for some sense of sanity in planning, organizing, and implementing lessons. Let's not forget that I was working with five-year-old students, many of whom had never been in a classroom setting before. Not only were they facing a major transition in their young lives by coming into a classroom of strangers and a six foot four, spiky-haired male teacher, but the expectations set before them were getting higher and higher.

These same expectations frustrated the teachers, and I found myself joining their ranks and throwing around the same complaint: "Things are being pushed down on kindergarten students by people who have never been in a classroom before!" True, the expectations for children in every grade level have been rising over the years but, instead of continuing to complain, I decided to take a different approach. To be blunt and fully honest, I don't think for a second that the curriculums or standards have caused a decline in classroom play over the years. I do believe teachers have more on their plates than ever before, but that shouldn't warrant an excuse for administrators or teachers to not create engaging learning environments. It just might take a little more creativity and hard work. Now, we teachers might not want to hear this, but I'm just going to say it: "If you aren't willing to work for it, don't complain about not having it."

Easier said than done, right? I've done my fair share of complaining about conditions in education over the years, and guess what? It never helped solve a problem. I learned very quickly from my mentor teacher, Mrs. Honor Trotter, that hard work is the only way to get what you want. She was better than anyone I had ever met before at facing problems and making tough decisions in the workplace.

When a problem arose, she'd always take the same approach. She would first take a step back, look at all the possibilities, and then go directly to the source to talk it out. I appreciate how lucky I was to learn from this woman who was amazing both in and out of the classroom.

Though I never mastered this practice as well as Honor, with her guidance, I started looking at my problems with new curriculums and standards in a much different way. I started challenging myself to think about how to help my students learn rather than complain about what my students couldn't master. As I shifted my perspective, I realized just how much I was doubting my students by taking a negative approach to the new standards and curricular expectations. By following the crowd of complainers, I wasn't truly believing in my students and their potential. Changes in education were forcing new expectations upon my kids, and there was nothing I could do about that. But what I could do was create new and different meaningful activities that would engage, encourage, and excite each young mind that entered my classroom!

That idea in a nutshell is exactly what I aim to do with this book. As you read through its pages, maybe you'll find that you're already doing or have done some of the ideas I share, and you've just let some games get shoved to the back of your closet. Or maybe you're feeling the stress of multiple changes in your building, and this is the spark you need to get your sanity back. Or maybe you're a new teacher who wants to begin a successful career filled with both effective learning and good fun. Whatever the reason, thank you for picking up this book and starting a journey that I'm confident will benefit your students in many ways. Let's play!

A TESTIMONIAL OF ADAM'S TEACHING STYLE

Adam visited our district in August of 2019 to kick off our year and inspire our early education teachers to explore their inner creativity. His time was spent with early childhood, kindergarten, and first grade teachers that he inspired to "change the game" for our youngest learners by incorporating more play-based and hands-on learning into their classrooms. Adam shared the message of how to create fun learning experiences in the classroom and meaningful ways to engage today's children from the start by creating a family-like classroom environment. Adam is engaging, passionate, and confident in his delivery, which inspires educators to want to create more fun experiences for their students. He promoted thinking-outside-of-the-box planning and student-centered approaches to learning in his PD. This message gave our teachers permission to transition away from traditional "sit-and-git" methods to exploration and play. This type of professional development is vital for teachers to continue to grow their practices each year to meet the needs of all children in their classrooms.

—Mrs. Jennifer Seykora, Principal

1

GIVING PLAY A PURPOSE

"**WHY PLAY?**" I'm often asked. This question usually comes from someone who has a mindset different from mine when it comes to developmentally appropriate learning. When that question arises, my answer is simple: "Kids need to play!" I always encourage the people asking to think back to their own childhood and primary classrooms. Most of the time, they recall sand tables, easels, hopscotch, puzzles, and more. Kids are kids, and whether we want to admit it or not, kids haven't changed. For example, take these two kids:

(Me in kindergarten, 1987)

(My son in kindergarten, 2017)

Nothing is really different about these two little boys. The one on the right is much like the one on the left. Both children enjoy doing things and love sharing new experiences with their friends. I've found that, just like in my own childhood experience, my two children learn more when they're engaged in what they're doing. They both do great in school and never contest the traditional style of teaching they regularly experience, but can true learning happen with this "sit-and-get" style? For some students, this type of teaching does result in learning. For others, it does not. Using a mix of the two teaching styles (sit-and-get and play-based) in your classroom can help address the needs of all your students.

Maybe you're thinking, "But wait a minute, Adam. I thought you preach that play-based teaching is the way to go?" Let's set the record straight here. I believe that play-based teaching is the key to getting children excited for learning about the world around them. However, there were times in my classroom when my students did sit for lessons and practice rote skills.

Still, after many years of my practicing the ideas you'll be reading about in this book (and because of the stories past students have shared with me), I know that the experiences I offered for learning the information I was required to teach helped make the learning last. When we teachers tie information to a meaningful and memorable experience, we can create a place where children love to learn, and the learning will happen naturally. Now think back to your own primary education. I'd be willing to bet that you can recall your learning while doing and experiencing things much better than you can recall your learning while sitting at a desk memorizing facts. Not much has changed when it comes down to the heart of why and how kids learn. Don't get me wrong. I'm well aware that society has changed, expectations have changed, and the world around us has changed. However, I truly believe that kids are still kids, and kids still very much need to play! My goal for this chapter is to help you define and start to visualize how this style of teaching can look in your own classroom.

DEFINING A PLAY-BASED APPROACH

For many of you, picking up this book might seem like the first step on a path to creating a play-based learning classroom. But what if I said you were wrong? What if I said you've been doing play-based activities in your classroom since you started teaching? You may not think so, but it's true: songs, dances, finger plays—properly understood, all these qualify as play-based learning. If we take a moment to look at the definition of play, I think you'd agree.

But before we do that, I want to stress that a play-based approach doesn't involve burning your teacher's manuals and saying goodbye to rigorous academics. Please don't make that assumption about my classroom or that of any other teacher who embraces play-based learning. As I will show over the course of this book, all the play that my students have done in the classroom has been tied in a multitude of ways to specific learning targets while still meeting their developmentally appropriate needs.

Now, back to that definition:

> **play** /plā/
> *verb*
> engage in an activity for enjoyment and recreation rather than a serious or practical purpose
> *noun*
> activity engaged in for enjoyment and recreation, especially by children

I'd like to focus on three important words in that definition: *engage, activity,* and *enjoyment.* Now ask yourself the following question: How many times a day do I do something in my classroom that has my students engaged, active, and enjoying themselves? My hope is that your answer is a high number! Next, I want you to reread the definition and ask yourself the question again, this time with a twist. Take any toys and manipulatives out of the equation. I'm talking all blocks, games, cards, train tables, kitchen sets, puzzles, pattern blocks, and cubes. Imagine that all these kinds of items have vanished from your classroom. Now I want you to answer the same question you asked yourself before. Chances are your number has dropped. Am I right?

The first time I ran through this same scenario in my head, my number dropped as well—but not as much as I thought it would. I found that when it came to my everyday routine lessons, a lot of sitting was going on and not as much hands-on play as I might have thought (for no other reason than I was following what my curriculum told me to do with no thought or creativity). Sure, I was doing some dancing and singing at the beginning of the day, but mostly I was at best hitting on only one of those three important words at any point in time. For example, my students might have been engaged in the lesson but were not actively enjoying themselves; other times, I could recall them enjoying themselves but not grasping the knowledge I was attempting to impart. In other words, they weren't engaged. Realizing I needed to do more to ensure that I was delivering the promise embedded in all three key words of the definition, I began systematically reviewing my classroom approach and each lesson. I made it my goal to incorporate activities, enjoyment, and engaged learning into as many day-to-day lessons as I could. The best part of methodically boosting the play factor was that I realized it really isn't hard to do at all.

In my school district, we had been using multiple curriculums throughout the day. The administration had chosen them because, among other reasons, each was research based and standards aligned. And while each curriculum was full of *what* I was to teach my students, none told me *how* to teach my students. Sound familiar? This goes right back to the quote in my introduction: "It's not about _what_ you teach but _how_ you teach that makes all the difference."

I'm actually quite grateful that the various curriculums didn't specify how to teach. Granted, I had to use specific terminology and teach specific skills, but thanks to an administration that trusted their teachers, and to curriculums that didn't dictate how to reach the targets, I was free to journey toward these destinations in ways that worked for me and my students. The purpose of this book is to show how you can adopt a play-based approach to any curriculum and successfully use that method to ensure that your students are engaged in activities and enjoying learning the content they need to meet the targets.

THE PLAY-BASED APPROACH IN ACTION

Let's take a look at a specific example of how I was able to do that. In one of our curriculums, my daily routine was to stand in front of my class and have my students repeat what I was saying. It sounded a lot like this:

> Teacher: "A says /a/ as in apple. /a/ /a/ apple."
> Students: "A says /a/ as in apple. /a/ /a/ apple."
> Teacher: "B says /b/ as in bear. /b/ /b/ bear."
> Students: "B says /b/ as in bear. /b/ /b/ bear."

We would continue this pattern for every letter of the alphabet day after day after day. For some students, this drill was very helpful. Some of my students had never been introduced to letters, and now they were constantly being exposed to the letters and their sounds. Great! But some of my students knew all their letters and sounds coming into the classroom and didn't need this daily routine. For them, it eventually got boring. And even for the ones that needed the practice, the basic script didn't engage them. They were not actively learning and eventually weren't enjoying themselves either.

But how, oh how, do we fix that? I couldn't just stop using the curriculum, but I knew I couldn't continue teaching this way either. So I decided to make a change. I have found that when you make any change, it's best to start simple. I knew from experience that engagement and enjoyment would come once I let my students be active. I started incorporating what I call partner play and started rotating different activities to keep my students engaged. The enjoyment followed naturally.

HAND STACK

Remember when we used to make playground decisions by going hand-over-hand with a friend on a baseball bat until one of us reaches the top? It's how my friends and I used to pick who went first in a game or which team got to bat first. I knew this was a concept that my kindergarten students could grasp quickly, so we used hand

stack to put a spin on our daily routine. Instead of simply sitting and repeating our letters and sounds while I flipped through flashcards, everyone was now partnered to stack hands.

Here's how it works. Let's pretend you and I are partners. We stand and face each other with our hands by our sides. You say "a" and put one hand out in front of you, palm down. I say "b" and place one hand on top of yours. You then say "c" and place your other hand on top of the stack. I then add my second hand on top on saying "d." This back-and-forth continues by taking turns moving our hands from the bottom to the top of the stack until we reach the letter z. To address additional standards, we eventually added in sounds and key words from our curriculum for each letter. I had my students engaged in an activity and enjoying themselves by adding a simple twist to practicing a skill I was required to teach.

It took some time getting it right, but my students got so excited about playing this game during our phonics routine that I saw them playing it even on the playground! It's so much fun in fact that I share

this game with ballrooms full of teachers at conferences, and they love it, too. To challenge the teachers, I have them play while saying the alphabet backward. If I can get large groups of adults actively engaged and enjoying themselves, it follows that the same will work for your students.

CRISSCROSS

Crisscross is an educational modification to the classic hand-to-hand game of pat-a-cake. Practicing the same phonics routine as above, students face their partner, but instead of stacking hands, they play pat-a-cake while saying "A-apple-/a/, B-bear-/b/, C-cat-/c/," and so on. My students loved every minute of this activity, and I no longer got blank stares from students who either weren't understanding these skills in whole-group lessons or were bored because the skill was too easy. I was reaching all my students by covering what was needed in a way that was fun for students at all levels of proficiency.

BACK WRITING

Kids have a natural desire to do silly activities with their friends. If we can tie that desire to a specific learning target, it's a win-win situation for teachers and students. I wanted to continue introducing new ideas to practice our letters and sounds in active ways. The students were having a blast with hand stack and crisscross, so I figured another activity would get them just as excited.

One morning as we were getting ready to do our daily phonics lesson, everyone jumped up and got together with a partner. I quickly said, "No, no, no. Everyone, sit down for today's lesson." I immediately heard moans and whines because they were so used to being active during these lessons. Much to their surprise, I told them not to sit down on their assigned spots but instead to sit down in a circle, facing the back of the person to the right of them. As quickly as the sounds of disappointment had started, giggles of anticipation took over. This time, the twist was writing the letters we said on the back of the person in front of them. By sitting them in a circle, everyone had a back "board" to write on and everyone's back was a board for someone else. The fun could not be contained!

Alternatives to everyday activities, such as number and letter writing, are an easy way to add a bit of joyous play to the simplest of tasks. Hand stack, crisscross, and back writing are just three simple examples of taking a standard, curriculum-driven lesson and making it anything but standard. Each is also an easy activity that can be adapted to address multiple skills. Just imagine the excitement in your classroom when your students get to play while practicing sight-word spelling, counting, skip counting, spelling their names, or any other rote skill. Silly, simple, and effective!

Three-person hand stack makes the game even more fun.

PLAYING WITH PURPOSE

As mentioned before, all the activities in this book are purposeful learning activities. Unfortunately, that truth isn't always easy to prove to people who don't have a play-based mindset. It is our responsibility for the sake of our students—and all future students—to prove to teachers, administrators, and parents that playing serves a real purpose in the classroom. I accomplish this important work in three ways.

TIE EVERYTHING TO A STANDARD

One of the most obvious ways to prove that play is meaningful and has purpose is to show that the activities are helping you meet the learning standards required of you and your students. True, many of the games and activities children play can look pointless to the untrained eye. But if we're going to shift the teacher mindset toward a positive view of play-driven classrooms, we need to help even the biggest naysayer believe in the power of play.

In schools these days, learning goals are driven by setting standards and then collecting data that measures student achievement against those standards. Play-based activities would appear to apply to the exact opposite of that mentality, but that's not the case in reality. If you have a reason why you're playing a game, it's not hard to find the corresponding standard that reflects the point of the play. I have found it a good exercise to literally label every board game, card game, and activity with the corresponding standards that students are tackling when playing it.

This labeling process has done two remarkable things for me in the classroom. First, it has helped me understand my standards better than any textbook I've read or training I've received. When I have an actual activity to tie to a standard, I recall the standard much better and even see what the standard writers were aiming for when they wrote the standard. Second, this process allows me to pinpoint learning standards for anyone who walks in my room and thinks my students are "just playing." As a proponent of the play-based approach, being able to redirect conversations from defending *whether* play-based activity is purposeful to the more positive action of sharing *how* this activity accomplishes learning goals creates a much better dynamic.

DOCUMENT CHANGE

Ever heard that saying "it's easier to ask forgiveness than it is to get permission"? I'm not saying you should needlessly go out of your way to do things without asking, but sometimes it can help you get your point across if you just do it. If you can do something and prove that it works, then who can tell you not to do it? This idea ties directly into my point about being able to meaningfully speak to the standards through play-based activity but takes it a step further. There is no doubt that I was able to do a lot of amazing things in my kindergarten classroom because I had administration supporting what I was doing. But their trust in me wasn't blind faith: I had proven over time that my style of teaching was working for my students.

I'm an advocate for play-based learning because kids need to play, but I'm also an advocate because it works. I documented the proof, as much as possible, in everything my students did throughout the day. So take pictures, record audio, keep portfolios, use assessment data—however you do it, just do it. Keep reading for advice about approaches for documentation.

ENCOURAGE VISITORS

My third and final point is simple: you can talk about play-based learning until you're blue in the face, but showing someone the power of purposeful play is what really seals the deal. To that end, the more people you invite into your classroom to see what you're doing, the easier it becomes for you to embrace a play-driven approach toward learning and be supported while doing it.

In the spirit of showing instead of telling, let me "show" you another lesson that won over a skeptical administrator, my principal. Had he just glanced through the window at the right time, all he might have seen was my students playing Plinko from *The Price Is Right*—probably not reassuring. But by inviting the administrator

Plinko is sure to liven up any lesson.

into my classroom, I allowed him to witness for himself that the activity was intentional in addressing a specific learning standard.

Let me set the stage for you, literally and figuratively. My students walked into the classroom one morning to find this board on our stage, covered with a large black sheet. (I have to thank my good buddy Kyle for using his amazing woodworking skills to build this amazing game board.) Immediately, the questions from my students started coming from left and right, the principal silently observing the scene.

"What is that, Mr. P?"

"What's under the sheet, Mr. P?"

To sell my students, I responded with the most exuberant tone of voice: "You, my friends, are going to love what's under that sheet. But I can't show you what's under it until we get through our lesson this morning. If you can complete the task I have for you to do with your magnet boards, then we can see what's under the sheet!"

Let me first put those magnet boards in context. The boards were part of a phonics program I was required to teach, which directed my students to do nothing more than repeat letters and sounds, then move magnetic letters around a board to match what they had just said out loud. That lesson on its own, while serving a very practical purpose, had very little activity. My students were rarely engaged and didn't enjoy it much—especially because this program would have them do the same lesson repeatedly for multiple weeks.

That bit of salesmanship suddenly made those magnet boards seem like the coolest new item I had ever used in our classroom. We went through our lesson as we normally would, with one exception. As my students completed each portion of the lesson, I walked around and dropped a wooden chip in each lap.

"What are these for, Mr. P?"

"I can't tell you that until we finish the lesson, but you're working so hard that I'm sure we'll be able to see soon."

The lesson continued with more engagement and enjoyment than ever before. The excitement was building. When they had completed the lesson, I unveiled the Plinko board with the enthusiasm of a magician revealing an object he had just made appear from thin air. As soon as I whisked the sheet off the board, the oohs, aahs, and screams of delight filled the room. They all realized what the wooden chips were for and lined up to take their turn dropping the chips in the board. One by one, my students released the wooden chips from the top of the board and squealed as they watched the disks bounce all the way down.

This successful lesson was proof to the administrator that I was teaching what the standards required me to teach but with a play-based approach. In fact, the high level of engagement and the reinforcement of the lesson that the anticipation of Plinko created meant that I wasn't only teaching phonics; students were learning phonics. My administrator was more than convinced that play could be effective in the classroom, and the kids even persuaded him to participate by dropping a chip. From that day forward, he not only let go of his skepticism but also became one of the strongest advocates for play-based learning we had ever had in an administrator in our district.

Plinko was yet another activity that I easily adapted to meet the needs of multiple learning targets. Rather than having fun simply dropping chips in, the chips could land in one of five different slots, each labeled with a visual representation of a particular phonics concept. When the chips fall into these slots, the students turn around and give the class an example of the concept (e.g., a letter blend). Trisha has adapted the board for use in her second-grade classroom by adding pictures of coins to the bottom slots. Her students take turns dropping two chips in, adding together the coin values of the slots where the chips landed, and comparing their amount to a friend's result. This game would be perfect for any recognition or comparison skill you're trying to develop in your students.

ENTER THE DOUBTERS

Throughout the chapters of this book, I'll cover more easy adaptations that you can add to your classroom routines with very little planning. I have no doubt that at some point everyone will question at least one particular adaptation. I know from experience that several of you have this or a similar concern: "Well, I have this one little boy who never participates in the lessons, and now you want me to have him up and doing hand games with a friend? That will just cause more problems!" This is a legitimate worry, so we'll pause here to address the concern being raised.

EXPECTATIONS INSTEAD OF RULES

There's one element that makes these adaptations possible and addresses the doubt: expectations. We couldn't have done any of the play-based activities in my room if it weren't for the high expectations I set for my students from day one. I purposely use the word *expectations* rather than *rules*. As the old saying goes, "Rules were made to be broken." It's inevitable. No matter your abilities as a classroom teacher, your students are going to break some rules from time to time. They are, after all, children. I let my students know from the first day that I understand mistakes are going to happen, but it's what we do to fix those mistakes that makes us the people we are.

Instilling high expectations at the start helped me focus more on the children and less on their behaviors. Even with five-year-old students, I was able to create and maintain a highly effective, play-driven learning environment that ran without a behavior chart. (What!? No clip chart in my classroom?) My students learned very quickly that our shared expectations far outweighed the rules. On the first day of school, I would let my students know that they were part of our new family, and I welcomed them with a copy of a poster that I'd made for them and that they got to keep as a reminder of our classroom expectations. We'd go over the poster every morning for the first few weeks of school until I felt everyone understood the importance of each word of the five expectations:

1. We show respect.
2. You before me.
3. We use manners when we speak.
4. Hugs, handshakes, and high fives are a must.
5. We choose kind.

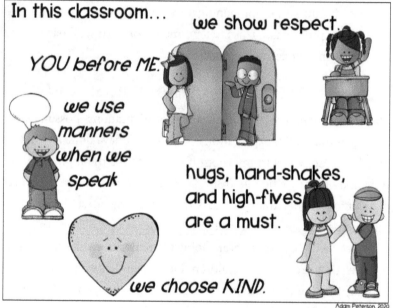

Clipart credit: Melonheadz Illustrating

The first expectation is as basic as it gets. In all situations, during all times of the day, we show respect to those around us. The second, putting others before yourself, comes from the lessons my parents taught me growing up. I taught my students to open doors for others, help others carry their books, assist others in cleaning up around the classroom, and so on. The third expectation reminded my students to use manners when speaking by referring to people with their names and titles. I also focused on polite ways to speak and ask for things. As part of our caring family, my students knew that offering a friend in need a hug, handshake, or high five can solve a lot of issues. Last, I taught my students to focus on being kind, always. This notion coincided with a worldwide kindness movement that I started at our school, called Make Someone's Day Yellow. If you and your school would like to learn more about this movement, visit www.makesomeonesdayyellow.com and follow #betheyellow.

I have given many talks across the country on my philosophy of expectations. Inevitably, someone in the audience comments that it's easier said than done. My response is always the same: "Well, maybe it is. But aren't we all looking for ways to make our jobs as educators easier?" Some audience members like that response more than others. In my view, kids are going to be kids, so creating rules is a losing proposition. Instead, I'm proposing that we treat students with respect and compassion and teach them how human beings should act. When a person has essential skills, such as showing respect and being kind, I believe those kinds of behaviors are far more important than whether that same person can sit still, raise his or her hand, or walk in a straight line. Belief in that concept is my one and only argument for establishing a system of expectations rather than rules.

If you buy into setting expectations, then why not make them easy to follow? For kids, simple means keeping everything as black and white as we possibly can. It goes back to the old adage "If it ain't broke, don't fix it." Why on the first day of school would we tell a five-year-old child to keep his hands to himself if he hasn't yet put his hands on someone else? The best way to avoid the problem is to never introduce the problem. The child who gets in trouble for constantly putting his hands on another student was going to put his hands on another student whether or not you have that rule in place.

GROUP WORK AND PLAY

Author Mia Sheridan said, "Friends are the family you get to choose for yourself." I took that quote to heart in my classroom every year, with every student. We focused a lot of attention on getting to know each other as much as possible on the first day of school and every single day forward.

All that groundwork helped me fulfill the next step in setting expectations for a play-based learning environment: creating a sense of family within the classroom. My students learned through the expectations I had in place that family is everything, and families work together. The family structure emerged most clearly in how I began to set my students up for success during game play in small groups.

Small-group work took up a great amount of time in our schedule. I wanted my students socializing as much as possible, and learning through play is the best way to do so. To achieve maximum individual and group productivity, I spent the first few weeks of school rotating my students into different groups while they played and learned in different stations. I observed and reflected and swapped until I felt that I had groups in place that could truly work as a family. Each group had to meet four criteria:

- Everyone works well together.
- Groups are a mix of girls and boys.
- Groups are a mix of academic levels.
- Everyone can be a leader.

Meeting these four criteria allowed me to create a comfortable learning environment for every student. Though there is no hierarchy of importance among the criteria, I looked for the first requirement immediately. Each group had to work together well enough that the students were able to use their time effectively while having fun. We've all had girls who are great friends in a social group but then try to take over when in a working group with their friends. The same goes for boys. I had years when all the kids got along well regardless of the situation, then other years when the smallest thing could cause a disruption. Creating groups of mixed genders was preferable, but the ratios varied according to the students in my class. Really, both the first and second requirements depend on the individuals assigned to your class.

The third criterion of mixing academic levels is relatively easy to meet with a variety of groupings. It is extremely important for us as educators to remember that no student is the best at every competency. I've taught students who read at a very high level but needed a lot of help with writing. I've also taught students who could rattle off math facts quicker than I could, but the same students had a hard time solving logic puzzles. With creating groups of mixed academic levels, the fourth factor naturally falls into place. You'll find that leaders emerge when their skills allow them to shine, and each students' strengths will be needed at some point during the school year.

Once I formed these family groups, they stayed in place for the remainder of the year. These were the groups that would play games and do small-group activities together. Whenever I needed the students to work in a group for any reason, all I had to do was call them by their group names. They knew immediately who they'd be working with. It saved so much time in the classroom—especially when we paired up with another class or if I had a substitute teacher who needed to put students in groups.

While my students were working in family groups around the classroom, I strategically pulled students of like abilities to my table for on-level learning in instructional groups, where we spent our time focused on developing needed skills based on assessment data. Meaningful data is such an important tool in education and small-group work, but some teachers feel they don't have time to assess, calculate, and compare data. I found an easy solution for that dilemma when I discovered ESGI Software. I used this software in my classroom beginning in 2012 and never looked back. With the ability to track my students' progress in real time, I could assess, compare, and group students in a matter of minutes to ensure that the instructional groups were learning what was required during any given week, lesson, or unit.

Learn more about
ESGI here!

So how did the typical day flow with whole-group, family-group, and small-group learning? I ran two main station blocks during the day that coincided with our main academic blocks. In the morning during our English language arts (ELA) block, I taught a whole-group mini-lesson on the current unit of study. After the mini-lesson, we spent the next hour in ELA stations. Family groups worked their way around the classroom playing different games and activities that met multiple standards we had already covered or were currently covering. While the family groups were learning together, I walked around the classroom and pulled students into instructional groups based on like skills from recent observations or assessments. It was as simple as saying, "I need you. Go get your things and meet me at my table." At the small-group table, we reviewed the day's mini-lesson for extra practice, played various learning games addressing a specific skill, or learned new material to meet added learning standards. I decided what to teach according to the skill levels of the students in each instructional group. In the afternoon, we followed the same type of schedule during our math block, as seen in the highlighted sections of my schedule.

Daily Schedule

7:50 Arrival/Morning Bins/Reading

8:15 Morning Meeting

8:45 Current Theme Story/Writing

9:10 ELA Mini-Lesson

9:20 Restroom/Snack/Reading

9:35 Recess

10:00 Story

10:20 ELA Stations

11:20 Restroom/Ready for Lunch

11:35 Lunch/Recess

12:10 Writing Mini-Lesson

12:20 Math Mini-Lesson

12:45 Specials

1:15 Math Stations

2:25 Pack Up/Dismissal

I am always asked two questions of concern about the family group and instructional group dynamic:

- What were the family groups doing while you were occupied with the instructional groups?
- How do you know the family groups were learning their skills?

My answers should not surprise anyone. First, when I was teaching the instructional groups, the rest of the students were busy learning through play in ways you'll read about throughout the rest of this book. They were completing activities that directly related to a lesson or unit we were currently studying. When they finished with those activities, they were given time to play with games and manipulatives in the area of the classroom where their group was assigned. The "have-to" activities (things they were required to complete) and "can-do" activities (things they could choose to do once the required activities had been completed) were purposefully set up for family-group work because the students were able to do these activities without assistance from me.

Second, I truly believe that kids learn more from each other than we give them credit for. I knew that the mixed levels of student abilities within each group would grant many opportunities for my students to help each other when I was busy with a different group of students. Not all students were able to complete the skills covered in each game in the same amount of time. All the students were on their way to reaching the goals that I had set, but their paths to get there might have been very different than those of their friends. To help them remember that it was OK to ask a friend for help, we had a much-used saying: "If you say it when you see it, it will stick inside your brain!" My kids followed that cue as an unwritten expectation to know how to ask for help. They understood that their friend couldn't simply give them the answer; the student asking had to repeat it.

If you find yourself asking similar questions of concern during any part of this book, just know one thing: my students were very much teachers to each other any chance they got. Whether they had mastered a skill and were helping a friend or they were seeking out the help of a classmate themselves, they were each learning something from the other through the games they played.

HELP WITH DOCUMENTATION

One final way I made sure that learning was going on during family-group time and that my students were held accountable was to have them document their own learning. You can do this in your own classroom in a number of ways. The easiest way to teach your students accountability is to always have them ask another friend to check their work. You can even lay out fun stamps or stickers to let the students mark their friend's paper after checking.

But what if they are playing games or doing activities that don't require a recording sheet or any type of paper? Taking pictures or recording video and audio clips for digital portfolios is a fun and fantastic way to let your students document the activities they've completed. My students loved using recording devices whenever they couldn't turn in some kind of physical record of a completed activity. For example, if a group of students was playing a game in which they matched letters with beginning sounds, I wanted to know that they did it correctly. Because of the game format, they had nothing to turn in to me. And they knew they were not to interrupt my small-group table to show me. Using an iPad or other device in the classroom, my students would take photos of their completed matches or record a video in which they told me about their matches. By using tools such as Google Drive or the app Seesaw, you can track and share the documentation of work and play that your students are doing on their own.

NEXT STEPS

Alright, are you excited to play? This book is full of engaging activities that will have your students learning in ways I've described above. As you read through these examples, keep your own teaching circumstances in mind, thinking about what you can do to create your own play-based activities to stimulate student learning.

Indeed, sometimes play can be accomplished through the way you're already teaching. Really, it can! If you refer back to the definition of play and refocus on the three key components—engage, activity, enjoyment—I think you'll see how easily you can create play-based activities. Try it now: Pick one dull lesson that you know you have to teach in your curriculum. (This exercise is more effective if you choose a lesson where students are sitting and not being very active.) Take that lesson, and just imagine how much better it could be with a bit of play-based engagement and activity. I guarantee that after you read this book and apply its principles your students will enjoy learning much more!

Rethinking your way of teaching isn't the easiest thing to do, but what's life without a good challenge? So I'm challenging you to the following:

- Allow yourself the time to read this book.
- Take any idea from this book and try implementing it in your classroom.
- Take stock of what goes well and explore how you can refine the play.
- Create your own play-based learning activity to enhance or replace a current lesson in your classroom.

And the greatest challenge of all? Do all of the above while remembering what it's like to be a kid! How much would you have benefited from purposeful play?

Challenges accepted? Then let's play!

2
OLDIES
BUT GOODIES

HUMAN BEINGS HAVE such a love-hate relationship with board and card games. Some of my biggest arguments as a child were with my sister and brother during heated games of Monopoly. Who hasn't experienced that, right? I love that game, but others can't stand to play it. My family plays board games all the time, and we've had our share of arguments from time to time, mainly because my wife is the most competitive person in the world. And my son inherited every bit of that characteristic.

All joking aside, we do love to play games at home, and Trisha and I both take this love of ours into our classrooms as well. I can remember playing many games with my family during my childhood, but the ones I remember most are the ones that allowed for a bit of creativity outside of the rules. Battleship was a favorite for me and my brother because how the game played out was entirely up to the players and where they placed their ships at the start of the game. We also enjoyed Operation because we would find random items around the house to place in the game board to see if we could pull them out without setting off the buzzer. Clue has always been a family favorite as well because it's different every time you play, and the game play is completely up to the individuals making the accusations. This type of creativity is what inspired the adaptations you'll read about in this section of the book.

BOARD GAMES YOU WON'T GET BORED WITH

In this section, we'll explore some of my favorite board games to use in the classroom. I'll highlight the ways I adapt them to teach multiple standards and show you how to do the same in your own classroom.

CANDY LAND

Candy Land is by far one of the easiest board games to teach to young learners. Why? The only requirements are matching colors and counting to one! Actually, sometimes a player has to count to two if a double-squared card is drawn. That's all your students really need to know. I love the light in my students' eyes when they quickly learn how to play this classic game, and I love watching them enjoy it with their friends.

In my school, I was never known for having an organized classroom, at least not in my closets or teacher area. I had a lot of storage, but the closet doors stayed shut because each shelf looked like it could be the star of its very own episode of the show *Hoarders*. I believe that if someone started a *Hoarders: Teacher Edition*, it would be wildly successful, and I would gladly star in the first episode. In one of my storage closets, several shelves were dedicated to board games alone.

On those shelves, Candy Land took up quite a bit of real estate. I absolutely hoarded copies of this game! I picked it up any chance

I got from yard sales, donations, and occasional store sales. If one was offered to me, I took it. You might ask why someone would need multiple copies of the same board game. Seems a little crazy, right? Wrong! I wasn't scavenging all these copies for the board part of the game at all. I simply wanted the cards. After I saw how quickly my students could learn to play Candy Land and how much they loved to do so, I realized I had to make this game last as long as possible in our classroom. Colors and counting, however, quickly got too easy; the board game was being used less and less. This is where all those extra copies came in handy. They helped me form the principle that would soon help me use all the games I had over and over again: Don't change the game; simply change the concept!

With this guiding principle in mind, I started going through all the boxes of Candy Land and pulling out the sets of cards. Because we had already played this game multiple times, each of my students knew how to play this game in small groups without assistance from me. I didn't want to abandon the game altogether, so I decided to throw them a little curve ball by changing up the cards to create a newfound sense of excitement with the same old game board.

Each week, I dedicated a portion of our school day modeling the new activities that would be available for my students during our scheduled station times. I would remove the activities from their station tubs and show them one after the other to my students, step by step. This display was always an exciting time because my students knew a bunch of brand-new activities were waiting for them to play with in stations that week. This was also a good opportunity to use some humor with my students and get a good laugh out of them by making them think I had no idea what I was talking about. By this point, they had been playing Candy Land for a week, so each group had already had a turn during stations. So imagine their surprise when I was modeling stations the next week and there in the tub for the puzzles and board games station was the same old Candy Land box.

"We already played Candy Land, Mr. P! You forgot to change the station tub!"

(Insert the uncontrollable laughter of five-year-olds.)

But my reaction was as serious as could be, and I hushed their laughter quickly. I pulled the game box out of the station tub as slowly and dramatically as possible. I treated the box as if it contained the most prized possession, the most coveted board game on the face of the Earth, something they had never seen before.

"Oh no, no, no, my friends! This may look like an ordinary Candy Land box, but this box contains a game unlike any you've played before. This box contains a game only found within the four walls of our classroom—a game that nobody in your family has ever experienced and nobody else anywhere in the world has ever played. Who wants to see what it is?"

(Insert the uncontrollable cheers and screams of five-year-olds.)

"OK, friends, let's take a look! Scoot back, sit in a circle, and prepare to see the most amazing board game you've ever seen!"

I opened up the box, laid out the game board, and pulled out the familiar-looking cards, being sure to hold them facedown.

"Hey! That's not a new game. That's the same game we already played."

We all have *that* student in our class, right?

"Wrong, my little friend. You may have played Candy Land before, but you've never played Candy Land like this! In fact, nobody has ever played a game of Candy Land like this. Your parents, grandparents . . . no single person has ever played a game of Candy Land like this before!"

As you no doubt have noticed, I was trying to sell the excitement of this "new" game as much as possible. With all eyes on me and all my students now sitting on their knees trying to peek at the cards, I slowly turned over the deck to reveal that a picture had been added to each card. Really, that was it. I had taped onto the cards next to the colored square the photos of my students that I had taken as usual on the first day of school. Screams of excitement erupted and smiles spread across faces immediately as the students tried to find the card with their own picture on it. Even *that* kid was excited about this simple change in the game.

I went on to explain that the rules to this new game, titled Candy Land Friends, were exactly the same as regular Candy Land, with one exception. In this new version, a player draws a card, then says the name of the friend on the card before moving to the colored space or spaces shown. Voila! Instant engagement and excitement created by an extra set of Candy Land cards and a simple twist. This modification can easily be made to meet the needs of your students and cover the standards you're working on. I changed the concept without ever changing the game!

Listed are some other skills I addressed by continuously creating different versions of the game by adapting the cards.

- **Alphabet:** Add uppercase and lowercase letters for a simple game for practicing letter identification.
- **Numbers:** Use numbers one through thirty to practice number identification.
- **Number sense:** Add dots, ten frames, and tally marks to practice recognizing numbers in different forms.
- **Names:** Print the first names of the students in the class to help students learn how to read and write their friends' names.
- **Sight words:** Add current sight words as well as high-frequency words from the current unit of study for students to practice reading skills.
- **Math problems:** Affix simple addition and subtraction problems to help students master basic math facts.
- **Rhyming pictures:** Add one simple, familiar picture per card for students to name rhyming words; add two pictures per card for students to tell whether the words rhyme with each other.

The possibilities are endless and endlessly exciting. My students couldn't wait to discover what game they were going to play each week, never realizing the amount of learning they were doing as they played!

CHUTES AND LADDERS

Chutes and Ladders is also an easy game to introduce to your students. Much like Candy Land, it's a game most kids have played, as it is one of the early learning games you typically see on the game shelf in any home with young children. While it is an easy game to introduce, it can be a tough game for children to play at first because of the layout of the game board.

The main skills of Chutes and Ladders are number recognition, counting, and number order. The third skill is the toughest for some children to master, but they have to know number order to make their way through the game. The changing direction of number order from row to row really throws off some students. Once learned, this game will help enhance the three math skills mentioned, and your students will love playing it.

As with Candy Land, I began making adaptations to use this game in various ways throughout the school year. The first step is realizing that you don't have to limit the way your students take turns by only using the spinner that comes with the game. When your children have learned the game with the original spinner, swap it out for dice, cards, or even customized spinners. Here are some examples to consider:

- Use your alphabet and number cards from Candy Land in place of the original Chutes and Ladders spinner. A simple color-coded key that you create allows your students to practice letter and number recognition, color matching, counting, and number order in one turn! On each turn, a player flips over a card, reads the letter or number, matches

Chutes and Ladders Key

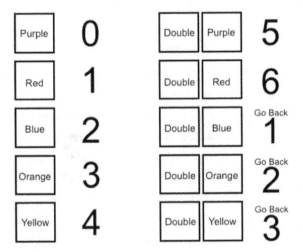

Chutes and Ladders key using Candy Land cards in place of the spinner.

the card's color to the color on the key, reads the number on the key, and moves that many spaces.

- Replace the spinner with various kinds of dice to help your students practice their addition and subtraction skills. For example, the sum or difference of two dice rolled on a turn can equal the number of spaces the student moves on the board.

- Substitute in modified spinners. For example, I found at Dollar Tree a pack of four spinners with the numbers one through eight. I kept one spinner as it was and used it in place of the original spinner. On two other spinners, I placed stickers above the numbers and used a marker to add letters to one spinner and numbers to the other. For these two spinners, I created a key—much like the color-coded key— that shows the number of spaces a player moves depending on the letter or number indicated on the spinner. On the fourth, I wrote current sight words. When players land on a word, they first read it, then move the number of spaces that matches the number of letters in that word.

HIHO! CHERRY-O

The HiHo! Cherry-O game rounds out the three that I usually see marketed for early learning. Like Candy Land and Chutes and Ladders, the basic version of this game is a cinch for kids to learn but helps develop an essential skill. In this game, children spin to add or subtract a number of cherries on their cherry tree. It's a great game for counting forward and backward by ones and twos. For a lot of students, counting backward in particular is a great skill to practice in itself. But what if you don't want to rely on the spinner to simply tell the player how many cherries to remove or place on the tree? Adding basic flash cards to this game provides students practice for not only counting but also number identification and math facts, depending on the type of cards used. Here are just a few variations to consider:

- **Numbers:** Players draw a card and say the number before spinning the spinner.
- **Dots, ten frames, and tally marks:** Students practice number sense before they take their turn at the spinner.
- **Names:** Make your own flash cards with the names of everyone in the class for students to read before spinning.
- **Sight words:** Players read the word, roll a die with operation symbols for addition and subtraction, then add or remove cherries equal to the number of letters in the sight word.
- **Addition and subtraction:** Students practice identifying numbers and solving simple equations to determine the number of cherries they add or remove.

OTHER GAMES TO CONSIDER

It would be impossible to go into detail on every board game I've used in my classroom in one chapter. That's where the skill of thinking like a teacher comes in handy. Adapting board games is as simple as blending what your students need to learn with how they enjoy learning it. Take a look at your game shelf and see how you could use my examples to adapt the games you already own. In my classroom, I also included many other board games that weren't as adaptable but still taught turn taking, strategic thinking, and multistep thought processing. You'll find a list below of the games we've used for these learning purposes while having fun. As you visualize each game, think of simple tweaks you could make to suit the teaching and learning in your classroom. By changing up the elements of game play, and by incorporating different content and addressing different standards, you can put a new spin on these games and keep them fresh throughout the year.

- checkers
- Sequence
- Connect 4
- Cootie
- chess
- Sequence for Kids
- Trouble
- Kerplunk
- Sorry!
- Sequence Letters
- Battleship
- Pop the Pig

There are so many more games I could list, but this is a good place to start. With the constant evolution of new and exciting games, you're sure to add to this list on your own as you continue teaching through the years.

MOVING PARTS = MORE FUN!

I'll never forget the year my sister got the game Mouse Trap for Christmas. We played it all the time. This basic game didn't require any strategy whatsoever, but the way the pieces moved when a certain trigger on the game board was tripped was mesmerizing. I remember us setting up the reactions in different ways to see if we could make the marble roll in different directions with different outcomes. This game of contraptions became a go-to activity for us because it combined our love of board games with the wow factor of moving pieces. This engaging combination has led me to include other games of a similar type in my classroom.

LET'S GO FISHIN'

Another classic, this game features fish that bob and sink in a battery-powered pond. Students love to play this game. However, most parents despise it because they can't stand picking up those little plastic fish from all over the house. That fact alone makes it likely that you'll acquire this game through a parent's donation!

Right out of the box, this is a game of color recognition and hand-eye coordination, plain and simple. Young children learn the concept of the game quickly but find it tough to master catching those little fish. Hand-eye coordination is a complex cognitive ability, and games that strengthen your students' visual and motor skills are great additions to your classroom. The swinging action of the fishing poles combined with the speed of the fish requires students to have to concentrate to hook a fish. To add to the frustration, students are continuously battling their friends, who are also swinging their fishing poles around the pond.

Because the game comes with only four fishing poles, teachers ask me often what to do when their students are working in groups of five or six. The answer to that dilemma is that you are the teacher, so you make the rules. Just give the players one fishing pole to share! This game is the perfect way to teach kids a necessary skill: taking turns. By putting out only one fishing pole, you eliminate the arguing over fish and you encourage your students to cheer for and support their friends.

When I first introduced this game, the rules were very straightforward:

1. One player holds a fishing pole and puts the other hand behind his or her back. (Using two hands tends to lead to cheating.)
2. The other players cheer for the friend trying to catch a fish.
3. The player fishing gets three attempts at catching a fish.
4. After three tries, the fishing pole is passed to the next player, and the turns repeat until all the fish are caught.

Played in this way, this basic game is now a station that the students will play for quite some time because it takes a while to empty that little pond.

You can also apply the rule of not changing the game but changing the concept to Let's Go Fishin'. Just as with Candy Land, my students would follow the station rules until I felt they were all comfortable playing it. Then, with a bit of selling, I would make this game new, exciting, and perfect for what we were currently learning in class. Don't overthink differentiation in your classroom. My students absolutely loved going for those fish all over again, thanks to this one little spin on the rules. And it doesn't need to be an elaborate change to rekindle the spark. My kids loved this game so much that I had to come up with ways to keep it in our station rotation, but because there are no cards to adapt I had to adapt the fish. At my local dollar store I bought packs of garage sale dots, those neon circle stickers, which happen to fit perfectly on the bottom of the fish. I labeled each fish with elements to develop different skills, and I instantly had multiple ways to surprise my students with new games! The following are just some of the additions I've made.

- **Alphabet:** Add uppercase and lowercase letters to make a letter identification game.

- **Alphabet memory:** I mixed and matched fish from the upper-case set and the lowercase set to create a memory game unlike any my students had played before. On each turn, my students caught two fish and kept them if they were a match.
- **Numbers:** Numbering the fish zero through twenty (there are twenty-one fish per pond) turns this game into an exercise in number identification. Once all the fish are caught, it becomes a number-ordering game as well.
- **Sight words:** Current sight words and high-frequency words helped my students practice reading skills.
- **Math problems:** Simple addition and subtraction problems, combined with the speed of this game, created a math fluency activity that my students enjoyed playing over and over again.

Fishing is a fun way to practice identifying and reading sight words

I made sure to collect multiple copies of this game any chance I could for a couple of different reasons. First, I wanted as many sets as possible to allow for multiple levels of differentiation. Regardless of academic skill level, all my students loved playing this game. Second, to change up the game, I would pull out fishing poles from the multiple sets I owned so that all the players had their own pole. One player in the group would flip a sand timer, and then they would all race against the other players to catch the most fish before time ran out. Adding this competitive edge to the game brought back the engagement in the most reluctant young learner.

HOT SHOT BASKETBALL

When I first started teaching, I took over for a teacher who had been in my classroom for many years prior to me. Going through the things she left behind, I noticed tucked away in the back of a closet a Travel Hot Shot Basketball game. It was in a tiny box and needed to be assembled to play. I didn't have time for that, so there it stayed in the back of my closet for quite some time. I let the size of the game and not wanting to assemble it stop me from using it. On top of that, I wasn't thinking like a teacher and was instead coming up with every excuse for why this game would not work in a kindergarten classroom.

I shook myself from that mindset one day and dug the game out of the closet. I put it together and started coming up with ways I could add this game to our station tubs. In its basic form, this game had no educational value other than taking turns and reading the numbers on the scoreboard in the rare instance a five-year-old could land the little ball into the hoop. Like the other games I've mentioned, I first modeled how to play this game using the included rules and quickly realized that the kids didn't care about the score. But they really loved launching the little ball from the catapult, so I adapted the game, creating sight-word basketball.

With the invention of at-home crafting machines, the die-cutting machine may seem like a thing of the past. Luckily, our school had an amazing parent-teacher organization that supplied us with all kinds of tiles for our die-cutting machine, so I used it quite a bit. With a circle-shaped tile, I cut out a bunch of orange circles. Using a black permanent marker, I drew lines on each circle to make it look like a basketball. I then labeled each basketball with a word from our list of past and current sight words. After running the freshly made basketballs through the laminator, our new game was ready to go.

Here's how the game is played:

1. One player draws a basketball from the deck.
2. That player reads the word on the basketball (or uses the phone-a-friend option) and then shoots baskets on the Hot Shot court, getting one shot for every letter in the sight word.
3. As the reader is shooting baskets, the other players are keeping track by spelling the word. For example, a student drawing the word *purple* gets six shots. On the first shot, the student's friends say "P." On the second, they say, "U," and so on.

This quickly and easily became a game my students went back to time and time again. It was a constant in our word work station in the classroom, and when my students finished their required activities in that area they almost always pulled out sight-word basketball. Just as with Let's Go Fishin', my students cheered for each other while taking turns reading and shooting. Without realizing it, they were practicing their sight words and having fun doing it!

Here are some other ways we modified and used the die-cut basketballs for specific skills to keep the learning alive with Hot Shot Basketball.

- **Numbers:** Students identify the number on the card and take that same number of shots.
- **Math problems:** Students solve simple addition and subtraction problems and use the sum or difference for the number of shots.
- **Syllables:** I added pictures of basic objects to the basketballs. Students clap out the syllables in the word drawn to get their total number of shots.

DEAL ME IN!

There is a quote by Randy Pausch that relates to so much in life, including to schools and classrooms: "We cannot change the cards we are dealt, just how we play the hand." The obvious meaning of living your life the best you can with what you have can easily be aligned to how you treat your students in class. We as teachers have no say in the students that are assigned to us, but it is our responsibility to do our best with them while they are there. The opportunity we have with these students is unique and will set the tone for their educational future. We need to embrace each of these young people as an individual and do our best to shape his or her young mind.

Now, let's take that quote from inspirational to a more literal meaning! The focus of this section is card games and the endless uses for them in the classroom. No matter what grade level you teach, you'll be able to adapt these games to fit your curriculum, teaching style, and students' interests.

GO FISH

When someone utters the words "card game" in an elementary classroom, the first game that comes to mind for most of us is Go Fish. I remember playing this game myself as a child, teaching it to my own kids, and using it in my classroom from day one. Go Fish in its simplest form is nothing more than a color-matching game. It is simple enough to teach to even the youngest children. The best part of this game is that it requires language. The constant asking and answering of questions encourages socialization, speech and language development, and turn taking. But why not take this simple game and turn it up a notch to make it something students go back to time and time again? With a permanent marker, stickers, and labels, I've created multiple versions of this game to use all year long.

Here are my suggestions for ways to breathe new life into this simple game:

- **Letters:** Uppercase and lowercase letters encouraged my students to practice letter identification in a different way. ("Do you have an orange fish with a capital *A*?")
- **Numbers:** Add numbers ranging from zero to whatever number your students are working on. ("Do you have a red fish with the number *36*?")
- **Sight words:** Current sight words, high-frequency words, and even names of classmates helps students practice reading skills. ("Do you have a blue fish with the word *can*?")
- **Math problems:** Simple addition and subtraction problems help students practice basic math facts in a new way. Move over, flash cards! (Player 1: "Do you have a purple fish with the sum of *2 + 2*?" Player 2: "I do not have a purple fish with a *4* on it. Go fish!")
- **Number sense:** With the simple addition of dot combinations, ten frames, and tally marks, my students were mastering number sense without ever filling in a worksheet. ("Do you have a fish with tally marks that equal nine?")

These are all easy ways to adapt the Go Fish cards you may already have in your classroom. Want an even easier way? You got it! I was wandering around my local dollar store one day and found shelves in the teacher aisle stocked with flash cards for practicing letters, numbers, shapes, addition, subtraction, and even geography. I'm not a big fan of using flash cards for drilling skills into kids' minds, but the store had a set of cards that included some fun, kid-friendly clip art with simple words. As I flipped through one of these sets of cards, I noticed a lot of words my students were constantly asking me how to spell. I immediately knew there was something I could do with these cards that would help my students learn their basic sight words. I grabbed two boxes and headed to the register.

Here's why. Go Fish is nothing more than a deck of cards made up of duplicates. By buying two sets of flash cards and shuffling them together, I created a brand-new version of Go Fish for my students to practice key reading skills. From that day on, I started taking a closer look at flash cards every time I saw them in a store. Flash cards for shapes, colors, letters, numbers, and more can all be turned into a Go Fish game just by buying two packs!

What's that you say? You don't teach kindergarten? Your kids are learning harder skills than basic reading? No problem! What simple skills do you teach that you might typically put on a flash card? Maybe you have flash card sets already stored in your classroom closets. Just acquire a second set, shuffle them together, and I guarantee your students will not only be more engaged playing Go Fish but also retain the knowledge much better than they would with the regular skill-and-drill of flash cards. This ask-and-answer style of game play will also reinforce essential speaking and listening skills that a lot of children might lack.

Classic card games have been played for years because they're easy and fun. Try adapting other classics, such as old maid and crazy eights, in the same way. For example, the objective of old maid is to not end up with the odd card. Simply add an unmatched flash card to the deck for players to avoid. And you can adapt crazy eights by adding math problems or key terms that the students must solve or define before playing a card. With some imagination, you can tailor any classic card game to the content you're teaching and the types of learners in your class—it's all up to you!

HIGH-LOW (VARIATIONS ON WAR)

When there's a game my own children and I enjoy playing at home, I often bring it into my classroom. Chances are it will have the same effect on my students. War is one of those games. I taught my own children this game at a very young age and we continue to play it to this day.

I am an avid collector of decks of cards. My wife and I buy them wherever we go, and family members donate old decks all the time to use in our classrooms. My students have used many a deck to play war, which is a good candidate for the principle of changing the concept but not the game. Obviously, by using regular old decks of cards, war challenges young learners to practice greater than/less than skills while also practicing number recognition. The only negative to using standard playing cards is that you're limited to numbers two through ten—that is, unless you're thinking like a five-year-old and adapting the game on your own.

Yes, you read right. After watching me repeatedly make changes to classic games, my students adapted this game on their own to challenge each other in a way that a basic deck of cards does not. One morning I was checking my students in and taking attendance in usual fashion. While I did this, my students spent their time socializing and playing games from our morning bins. As I chatted with a couple of students, I overhead two of my boys playing war. I usually included the game in our morning bins because the students loved playing it. It also encouraged socialization and communication first thing in the morning.

This particular morning was a little different, because I heard the boys saying numbers that are not found in a regular deck of cards. I was hearing things like "Twelve is greater than seven!", "Sixteen is greater than thirteen!", and "Twenty is greater than five!" I wandered over to where the boys were playing to try to figure out what they were doing. I thought maybe they had assigned values to the face cards or come up with rules of their own. To my surprise, their thinking was way ahead of what I expected. These two creative little boys had changed the game by each laying down two cards and adding them together. One sum battled against the other sum to determine who had the greater number. Wow! I was so impressed. Talk about a proud teacher moment. As Maria Montessori said, "The greatest sign of success for a teacher is to be able to say, 'The children are now working as if I did not exist.'"

I quickly had these two boys teach the rest of the class their new variation, and this teachable moment led me to a principle I never thought I'd believe in: Buy all the flash cards! By using plain old number recognition flash cards, I can accomplish the same thing the boys did, but my options for high sums are even better. With sets of addition flash cards, my students are solving predetermined problems to find a sum for battle. But why stop at sums? Here are some other ways you could use flash cards to create a new theme for war.

- **Subtraction:** Lay down two playing cards and battle with the difference, or use subtraction flash cards.
- **Letters:** Use alphabet flash cards, assigning values to the cards based on their order in the alphabet. For instance, an *M* beats a *K*. Or have students name a word that begins with the letter they (or their opponent) lay down. The first player to say a word wins that battle.
- **Sight words:** Using basic sight-word flash cards, students first read the word on the card they play, then the player with the longer word wins the battle. This is one of those situations where you'll need to think like a teacher, as many familiar sight words have the same number of letters.

These war adaptations will definitely have your students learning through play, but I want to share another way to adapt this simple game by tying it to multiple skills with a game we call Syllable War. My students were struggling with learning and practicing counting syllables in words. The skill just wasn't sticking with most of my students, regardless of the ways I tried to teach it. Because nothing seemed engaging for them, I thought adding a twist was exactly what they needed. In addition to our current study of syllables in our phonemic awareness lessons, we were practicing our greater than/less than skills in math and learning about animals in a themed unit of study. I decided to blend the three together in a multidisciplinary approach.

I used animal clip art from our study of land and sea animals to create giant playing cards. I put the name of the animal on each card as well to ensure that my students were learning the terminology and using more advanced language when naming the specific animals. For example, one card showed an anaconda, not a snake. We dealt out the new deck of cards like regular playing cards and began the game of war. Each player laid down a card but, instead of comparing numerals, the players clapped out the words to find the number of syllables to compare.

"An-a-con-da has four syllables!"

"But-ter-fly only has three syllables."

"Anaconda wins!"

Just like that, engagement increased with this basic game, and my students were learning animal names and syllable skills much better than before.

If you're going to try war, or any game in which numbers are compared, I highly encourage you to switch up the rules of winning. In my classroom, I noticed a trend when it came to number comparison with greater than/less than skills. My students were mastering the concept of greater than much faster than they were of less than. To help with this issue, we changed the rules of war so that the lesser card beat the greater card. Flipping the orientation for winning may seem minor, but it will have a big effect on your students, who must now focus on a different skill.

THINKING OUTSIDE THE DECK

My good friend and play-based learning guru, Dr. Jean Feldman, has come up with some of the most amazing, easy-to-use ideas I've ever adapted to my classroom. I've used a ton of her stuff over the years to enhance learning, and I'll never forget what she said to me once when I asked about presenting some of her ideas: "Teachers are the best pirates. We beg, borrow, and steal so many ideas!" She gave me the go-ahead to share whatever I liked, and I promised I'd give her credit. With the ever-changing world of online idea sharing, that practice is an important thing for all of us to remember. Give credit where credit is due.

Unfortunately, some games have been adapted multiple times over the years, and sometimes it's hard to find the source. I wish I could find the person responsible for creating the first version of the game I'm about to share because I—and other teachers who have introduced it to their classroom—always say the same thing. Our kiddos love it! This game is very different from the activities mentioned so far in this book because it is completely team based. It isn't a you-against-me game like most board and card games. Instead, it is a game played by everyone in the class at the same time with a common goal. The goal is to do better as a class each time the game is played by collectively becoming more fluent in whatever skill you choose to center the game around.

CIRCLE-TIME CARD GAMES

Here's how it works: find a container, add some flash cards, add a couple of themed cards, sit all the students in a circle, and see how quickly the class can empty the container of the flash cards. Each player reads the card he or she pulled and passes the container to the next player in the circle. If someone draws one of the themed cards, everyone says the predetermined phrase and that player's cards all go back in the container.

Sound confusing? Let's break it down with a specific, themed sight-word game that was a favorite of my students: Brains! The sight words were printed on fun, kid-friendly zombie-clip-art cards, and the key phrase was printed on an additional number of cards. To make this game even more fun, the container holding the cards was a brain-shaped gelatin mold I happened to find at a dollar store.

To play Brains, my students took turns pulling words out of the container. Each player read the word on the card, asking a neighbor for help as needed, then passed the container to the next player in the circle. If a student pulled out a card with the key phrase, everyone stood up, put their arms out in front of them, and said, "BRAAAIIIINNNSSS!" in their best zombie voice. The student who pulled that card would add his or her cards back to the container, and play resumed with the next player drawing a card. Play continued until the container was emptied. As you can probably imagine, I could count on this game for instant engagement whenever I pulled the brain container out.

Find more amazing clip art like this from Melonheadz Illustrating.

Here are some other versions of this game that I have made that could be adapted for letter recognition, sight-word practice, number identification, or any other skill.

- **Oh My, Apple Pie!:** Apple-shaped printed cards go in a pie tin, with some cards having sight words and some showing a picture of an apple pie. When a pie card is pulled, everyone shouts, "Oh my, apple pie!" Then the word cards go back in the pie tin.
- **Spider, Spider, Web!:** Cards with spider clip art are drawn from a Halloween-themed bag. Some cards have a web printed on them. When a web card is pulled, everyone shouts, "Spider, spider, web!" while pretending to pull spider webs off their head.

- **Freeze!:** Snowflake-shaped cards, or cards with any winter-themed clip art, are put into a stocking hat. When a freeze card is pulled, everyone freezes in place until the teacher counts down from three.

Find some fun, editable games here!

To see more games like these that I have created and made available, scan the QR code. You'll find variations of the same game, which include editable cards that you can modify to create games that address your skill of choice.

BASEBALL CARD GAMES

I have learned a great deal about keeping play alive in the classroom from my good friend and fellow kindergarten teacher, Kurt Schwengel. Kurt is nothing less than a genius when it comes to creating lessons and experiences for children based on their interests. He even wrote his own curriculum, *Rock and Roll Kindergarten*, which is loaded with these types of experiences. Kurt presents to teachers around the country on this subject, so I don't want to ruin any surprises. Let's just say his classroom is transformed into a bowling alley, golf course, construction site, and more throughout the year!

During one of his sports units, Kurt uses baseball cards as a manipulative to replace worksheets, teddy bear counters, and preprinted curriculum pieces. Instead of cutting and gluing pictures to practice sorting skills, or simply sorting bear-shaped counters by color and size, Kurt's students sort baseball cards. The best feature about this activity is that it has differentiation built right in. Students can sort by team name, uniform color, uniform numbers, player names, and more.

Kurt doesn't stop at sorting with these decks of cards though. I've seen them used to create custom bingo games, writing centers based on player names and statistics, math centers using the statistics, and many other activities that students love. Find more from Kurt, including a huge collection of themes and games, at www.rockandrollkindergarten.com.

FINAL THOUGHTS

Don't be afraid to try something new in your own classroom when it comes to classic card games, and don't hesitate to use your own creativity to develop custom games for your students based on their interests and yours. The simplicity of play and the interaction with peers will breathe new life into your classroom as well as their study habits. Kids are always looking for excitement, so if we can take a common game and make it feel special, we will have students who are excited to learn the information we put out there!

UPPER-GRADE EXAMPLES

The examples for board games I have shared so far are tailored to the kindergarten and primary levels, but it is easier than you think to make these games work at higher grade levels as well. Let's jump all the way to high school for an example that would work across many of these games.

Imagine you're a high school chemistry teacher whose students are struggling to remember the names of the elements on the periodic table. Bored to death with textbook studying and memorization activities, your students would be more than interested in practicing their element symbols when they see you pull out a copy of Candy Land, Let's Go Fishin', Hot Shot Basketball, or Chutes and Ladders! No study technique you've tried before will match up to letting your teenage students relive their childhood while learning the standards you're trying to teach them. Engagement will surely soar in your classroom because students aren't merely looking at elements on a chart but are seeing the symbols on a Candy Land card they've drawn or on the bottom of a plastic fish they've hooked. Think of the laughter you'd hear as they spell the names of elements while shooting for two in Hot Shot Basketball or matching element symbols to numbers on a key to move through Chutes and Ladders.

Card games are also easy to adapt for the upper grades. I'm sure there are many ideas you can come up with to adapt war for your own students that I can't even begin to dream up, but I did come up with one for the social studies teachers. If you teach US history, then I'm sure you have, or can find, flash cards of the fifty states. (I know that my daughter had flash cards in fifth grade showing outlines of the states, which she had to identify.) Take two decks of those cards, shuffle them together, and you have a game. Two or more students flip over a card, recalling the number order their states were added to the union. The highest number takes the cards.

What are your favorite games? More importantly, what are some favorites of your students? Use these answers to begin putting your own twist on games that will engage and excite your students in ways that'll make them love learning in your classroom. Take your curriculum, your current standards, and your current theme, and put them on cards for practice or for a review game. Your students, and you, will be glad you did. I'd love to see and hear your ideas! Share your own board game and card game adaptations on social media by tagging @teacherslearn2.

OUTSIDE THE CLASSROOM, INSIDE THE SCHOOL

Not all children have the same opportunities to play at home. As Dr. Jean mentioned in the foreword of this book, many factors weigh in on the amount of time children actually have to just be kids. As educators, we can help by sending home activities that encourage play, but there is no guarantee the kids will actually do them. So what if you could ensure that children are playing outside of the regular school day? I give you the after-school game club!

During the 2018–2019 school year, Trisha and her team launched an amazing new club at school. They invited all the second-grade students who were interested and had parent permission to stay after school once a week to play board games. As a new club, they had no idea what to expect in terms of interest or attendance, or if it would even be worth continuing once they got started. Their questions were quickly answered when over 55 percent of the second-grade students returned their permission slips! The main reasons even more didn't sign up was because of transportation issues or previous after-school commitments. The game club was a go!

The teachers had originally planned for the activities to take place in the classrooms of the second-grade teachers, but the club had to be moved to a gym or larger space to accommodate the unexpectedly high number of students. I visited the game club a couple of times, and it was quite a sight to witness. I was amazed not only at the number of kids in the room but mostly by their engagement in a wide variety of games. The students were socializing and learning with their friends and teachers, all while playing board games, card games, and movement games, many of which would typically take too much time to play in a classroom setting. Setting up a similar club at your own school can be very easy to do. You just have to find the right team to create it, gather as many games as possible, invite your students, and play!

3
HANDS=ON FUN!

PSYCHOLOGIST AND SCHOLAR Peter Gray said, "In social play, children learn how to negotiate with others, how to please others, and how to modulate and overcome the anger that can arise from conflicts."

The term "just play" is my least favorite to hear when it comes to play-based learning. Kids are never just playing, yet some people might believe that's all they're doing in an area such as a play kitchen. In those play spaces, children are working on many age-appropriate developmental skills. Socialization, communication, speech and language, sharing, and turn taking are just a few of the important areas of child development that a dramatic play area encourages.

Indeed, it is my sincere hope that one day every primary classroom will once again be graced with the presence of a play kitchen! There's something so eye-catching and imagination-inducing about walking into a classroom and seeing a matching wooden refrigerator, stove, sink, and cupboard, fully stocked with a large assortment of play food and plastic pots and pans. These pieces of furniture are far more than an area of the classroom for children to just play.

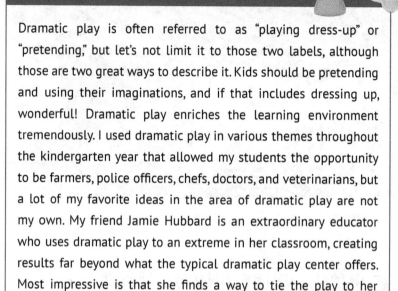

DRAMATIC PLAY WITH A PURPOSE

Dramatic play is often referred to as "playing dress-up" or "pretending," but let's not limit it to those two labels, although those are two great ways to describe it. Kids should be pretending and using their imaginations, and if that includes dressing up, wonderful! Dramatic play enriches the learning environment tremendously. I used dramatic play in various themes throughout the kindergarten year that allowed my students the opportunity to be farmers, police officers, chefs, doctors, and veterinarians, but a lot of my favorite ideas in the area of dramatic play are not my own. My friend Jamie Hubbard is an extraordinary educator who uses dramatic play to an extreme in her classroom, creating results far beyond what the typical dramatic play center offers. Most impressive is that she finds a way to tie the play to her rigorous academic standards and is able to prove its benefits by doing so. Jamie can share about her success with dramatic play much better than I can, so I'll let her tell you about her passion in her own words.

WHAT IS DRAMATIC PLAY?

What is dramatic play, you ask? Only the best form of play for our students! Dramatic play is imaginary play, where students might imitate any number of a range of social situations or roles. They might play dress-up and center their play around an outfit or use that kitchen for props to facilitate the activity, but whatever they do they are engaged in pretending. Dramatic play allows the child the opportunity to become a doctor or firefighter or teacher, among an entire host of other personas, but it also allows for great conversation, vocabulary building, learning, and maintaining self-regulation skills. Teachers who create play experiences based on learning standards will also see skill building in these areas come alive. And please do not forget the story retelling that can happen in an intentionally set dramatic play area. The opportunities for student learning are endless!

Dramatic play has always been an important concept to me because of the student dynamic that I have had in my classroom through the years. My prekindergarten class was part of the Voluntary Prekindergarten Program created to aid at-risk students with early intervention. These students often have never had the opportunity to visit a pumpkin patch, farm, airport, fire station, or many other places. I decided long ago that I would bring these places to my littles, because they might not have the chance to visit them outside of our school doors. That is my why. Why go over the top? Why spend Friday nights or Sunday afternoons in my classroom, creating learning spaces that most people shake their head at? Why go to Dollar Tree and Target 979 times a month to get one more pack of tiny pumpkins or more ink—again?

Because the littles.

The littles deserve learning experiences that will begin their educational careers in an exciting, fun, engaging way. They are my why.

In my own prekindergarten classroom, I loved to use my dramatic play area as an extension to the learning that we were already doing with our curriculum. I would build the area around the overall theme that we would be discovering, then create the activities within dramatic play based on the standards and skills that I wanted to target. I have brought learning to life through transformations during studies of fall, community helpers, families, animals and their habitats, holiday traditions and customs, winter, and so many more themes.

My favorite transformations have been the farmer's market with pumpkin patch, airport with beach destination, veterinary clinic, and flower shop. In these transformations, I included standards-based activities. For instance, in the farmer's market, we explored the math standards of sorting based on more than one attribute, counting one to ten objects, 2D and 3D shape identification and exploration, and number identification, along with recognizing currency and its purpose. During the airport with beach experience, my students were meeting goals and standards that addressed writing, letter and sound connection, letter recognition and number identification, sorting by size, ways things move, family customs, wants and needs, and money and direction words, to name a few.

English language arts standards might be, but are not limited to, writing, labeling, connecting letters to letter sounds in reading and writing, and learning and using new vocabulary words based on stories and books read and included in dramatic play settings. Math standards are covered in simple ways during these transformations as well. Your students can count and sort items found in the dramatic play area. If you're setting up an airport like the images I've shared, bring in pieces of luggage for the students to count, sort, and use for size comparison and ordering. Dramatic play transformations are often already heavily grounded in social studies and science standards without your having to work to add more experiences, but those areas can always be specifically addressed as well, as needed.

I hope my love for dramatic play shines through and that my whys motivate you to set some stages for your own students' experiential learning. Now, go build something fabulous and watch your students' playful spirit bring dramatic play to life!

—Jamie Hubbard, Rutherford County Schools

Students love to write and check airline tickets.

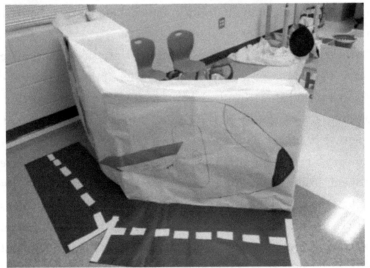

PLAYING WITH FOOD

The highlight of the play kitchen for my kindergarten students was always the absurd amount of plastic play food that would pour out of the cupboards when they were opened. I took any and all donations of play food, and it really added up over time. Eventually, I started adding the Melissa & Doug wooden play food sets into the mix, and the excitement for pretending grew even higher. There was no shortage of stuff in my play kitchen, but the substance wasn't always on point. Yes, my students were developing their social skills and playing at a developmentally appropriate level, but I knew there had to be more that I could do for my students.

I started scouring stores trying to find play food that offered greater opportunities for learning, and I found some great products that included food with alphabet matching, number matching, counting games, and more. But great products sometimes equal expensive products. As a teacher on a budget, I did buy a couple of these products but found it hard to justify spending a ton of money on them. Instead, I got a creative itch and started making my own versions of some of these games using things I had around my house and classroom. This is nothing new; teachers have been creating their own games for years from scraps of felt and old craft kits. It's what we do best. Still, I didn't want to ditch the regular plastic play food I already had, so I found a way to add a learning twist to them as well.

SORTING

Plastic play food comes in many different colors, shapes, sizes, and types. I've noticed in my classroom that when children see a box full of play food, automaticity takes over and sorting happens naturally. But I wanted to amp up this basic skill, so I took a quick trip to the local dollar store and found multiple baskets and containers in various colors and sizes. After a little work of typing, printing, and laminating some fun and colorful food labels, I had a new way to have my students practice their sorting skills, not to mention my classroom kitchen was much more organized, with all the items sorted by fruits, vegetables, breads, cups, bowls, spoons, and more.

SHOPPING LISTS

With some food clip art and the help of Google Slides, I started adding a touch of reading and writing to my play kitchen for next to nothing. By using Slides, PowerPoint, Word, or plain notebook paper and the copy machine, I created various lists of items my students had to find or shop for in our kitchen. The lists were simple, with pictures of food to find, collect, and cross off. I then added A-to-Z shopping lists, encouraging my students to find items in our kitchen that started with each letter of the alphabet. Numbered lists required my students to find one, two, three, or any number of a certain item to practice their counting skills as well. Soon my students were filling their dollar-store shopping baskets with food from a list, and they even started writing lists for each other.

GROCERY STORE

Kids love to pretend to shop. Trisha and I spent countless numbers of hours with our own kids when they used to set up their play kitchen in the basement and assign made-up prices to their food products. Add in my daughter's pretend shopping cart, a toy cash register, and some play money, and we had a full-blown grocery store running full-time in our basement playroom at home! As our kids grew out of playing with those items, I would slowly transfer the goods from our basement to my classroom kitchen. The kids didn't mind. Since both my wife and I taught at the same school, they spent plenty of time in my classroom and could still play with their own toys. It worked out nicely because my son and daughter had already laid out the necessities with the items from home, so my students were adding prices to classroom items and playing store in no time at all.

Counting money isn't a standard taught in kindergarten anymore, but I believe in exposing children to higher levels of learning any chance I can. I printed off pretend price tags and added them to the baskets in our play kitchen. This enhancement allowed my students to use the play food, shopping lists, and reusable shopping bags to shop for food, read prices, and check off lists.

STANDARDS-BASED PLAY SNACKS

While my students absolutely loved playing with our regular plastic play food in the ways mentioned before, I wanted to find a way to put even more purpose into our play food. We have a teacher-supply store near our school, with an impressive department focused solely on learning through play. I was wandering through their play food area one summer and found some amazing items. The company Learning Resources had released a series of purposeful play food called Smart Snacks, and they are, in my opinion, awesome!

These play food sets take classic, plastic food and put an educational twist on them by adding basic skills to the toys themselves. With these added to our kitchen set, my students were now matching uppercase letters to lowercase letters printed on popsicles. They were matching numerals to numbers with ice cream pops and colored coatings of different colors. Color matching and sorting became even more fun than before with small plastic cupcakes and color-coded muffin tins.

A big part of being a teacher is using resources that are readily available to you. Another part is creating things for your classroom as cheaply as possible on a small budget. Though I was fortunate enough to be able to purchase some of these sets for my students, I'm much more a fan of the DIY toys and games I can create by myself or with others. Using the more costly food sets as inspiration, I began searching dollar stores for supplies that I could use to make my own.

With a little creativity, I was able to grow my kitchen set with some other new purposeful items, which my students absolutely loved.

POPCORN PONG

To create a simple activity that I could use to reach multiple standards, I bought some plastic popcorn buckets and ping pong balls, then applied some basic number labels to the popcorn buckets. My students practiced their counting skills by placing the correct number of popcorn pieces (ping pong balls) into the buckets. Placing dice at this center as well allowed my students to roll, add, and place ping pong balls in the buckets based on the sum. The students could also easily practice subtraction by removing popcorn pieces from the buckets.

FELT POPS

I bought from my local dollar store some colored popsicle sticks that on their own are perfect for color-sorting activities. I also bought some felt in the same colors and cut two sheets of each color into the shape of tall popsicles. I then used a hot glue gun around the edges of the pairs, except the bottom, to create a popsicle sleeve. My students could then practice matching colors by sliding the felt popsicles over the popsicle sticks of the same color. With the addition of lowercase letters on the popsicle sticks and uppercase letters on the felt popsicles, I created a new letter-matching game with this same activity. I also made a number-sense game by putting dot combinations on the sticks and numerals on the felt. What's great about all these activities is that the popsicle sticks come one hundred to a pack and felt can be bought fairly cheap. Using only one set of materials, the options for differentiation are many.

BOX PUZZLES

My family and I eat a lot of cereal, and my kids are granola bar super fans. Together, we generate a lot of empty cardboard boxes. We do recycle at our house, but I started doing more reusing as well. Environmental print is one of the first things children learn to recognize and read on their own, so I wanted to create an activity that takes advantage of this early reading. I began removing the fronts from the boxes and then cutting those fronts into puzzle-shaped pieces. I laminated the pieces and stuck them in some colored baskets in the play kitchen. My students were excited beyond belief. Seriously, the cereal box turned puzzle became one of their favorite kitchen items to play with!

If you're not an avid cereal eater, what other types of boxes or containers could you save to create these same types of puzzles? Store logos, restaurant names, and so on—anything that includes some letters or numbers—are great sources of environmental print. If you can't get your hands on actual containers and packaging, go online to print familiar logos onto card stock, which you can then cut into puzzle pieces and laminate. Your students will love working puzzles that create images of their favorite fast-food joints and other places they know around town. In this situation, and so many others, never forget the power of asking for help. I've had a ton of luck with sending out emails or notes asking for donations of different boxes for puzzles I hadn't yet been able to create.

These activities are just a few ways that my students have practiced key skills while playing in the kitchen area of our classroom. But I didn't press those activities on them. I am a big believer in letting kids be kids. They love to use their imagination, and it is our responsibility to not only allow it but encourage it. Giving my students the opportunity to imagine themselves as chefs, cashiers, moms, dads, grandmas, grandpas, and pets (yes, they love to pretend to be dogs and cats) brings out the individual personality in each of them. Even my most shy, quiet students would come alive in the play kitchen because it was their opportunity to be little without the academic pressures of the learning process. They were learning to communicate, to share, to use manners, and so much more. Please join me in shouting from the school rooftops, "Bring back the kitchen sets!"

BLOCKS AND CARS

"The creation of something new is not accomplished by the intellect but by the play instinct." These wise words of Carl Jung are demonstrated every day in the classroom setting. When we take a step back and just watch our students be kids we are more able to see their natural instincts take over. Allowing your students time to be creative in various ways gives you the opportunity to observe, collect data, and record findings you might not otherwise see in your classroom.

I want to tell you a powerful story of student success in a struggling learner. For the sake of privacy, I'll refer to this learner as Elle. Elle came to my classroom with very few skills that could be considered academic. At five years old, she couldn't count beyond five, couldn't recite the alphabet beyond the letter *c*, didn't know a single letter of her own name, let alone write her name. Yet despite all the deficits holding her back academically (from a standards-based perspective), she showed amazing abilities in many other areas. Her ability to visually recognize similarities and differences in objects and pictures was beyond what was expected of a child her age. She could work a puzzle and solve problems with very little help from others as well. When it came to things not measured on a standardized assessment, Elle passed with flying colors and amazed me on a daily basis.

I'd be willing to bet that you have encountered students like Elle in your teaching career, too. Students who you know can do amazing things yet fail miserably when it comes to assessments. Students whose innate ability to explore, visualize, and create will take them far in life but who might not be anywhere near the top of the class according to academic standards.

This section is for those kids!

I'm going to share with you some of the activities that allowed Elle and other students like her to shine and excel in my classroom. Every student has talent in one area or another, and it is our job as teachers to recognize that talent, expose it, and use it to build up other skills. That's what I did with Elle, and it worked wonders. I'm not saying I did anything magical or outstanding; I only helped her to feel accomplished and helped her recognize her own abilities the way I had already.

I first noticed Elle's talents while she was doing what children do best—play. Her favorite area of the classroom was our blocks and cars area. There, I was able to witness my students building, sorting, designing, engineering, and so much more. This was one place in our classroom where they truly got to be kids. They learned in ways that were natural and fun and meaningful to them. (I can still remember the block area of the kindergarten classroom from my childhood!) When past students visit my classroom years later, it's one of the things they always mention. I can always tell that a part of them wants to head over there and begin building right alongside my current kiddos.

There's something special about those giant, solid wood blocks! They're the type you see only in classrooms and at children's museums, and kids—and I, I admit—crave time to use them. At the beginning of each year, my students would flock to the block center when we first started exploring the areas of the room, and for the rest of the year they always filled that area up during times of free-choice play.

But, like most kids, my students began craving more. In this case, I was OK with the requests because my students were showing a love of learning that I knew would continue to grow after they got what they were asking for. It wasn't long before I started hearing questions such as "Mr. P! Do you have any trucks or cars we can use in the blocks?" and "Mr. P! We're building a zoo, so can we bring the stuffed animals from the kitchen and use them in the blocks?"

My response was always "Yes!" But that wasn't the only response I gave. I challenged them to tell me—or better yet, show me—how they planned on using these things in combination with the blocks. Before I knew it, the blocks were no longer just blocks. They were parking garages, ramps, racetracks, construction sites, cities, and zoos. The collective imagination of my students ran wild; I was seeing more creativity than ever before.

I looked through closets and storage drawers for other items that would breathe new life into our blocks. I had a crazy number of items out for use during math lessons and centers, but my closets were still overflowing with teddy bear counters, pattern blocks, colored tiles, and linking chains. I literally had to catch the cubes and counters spilling out every time I bumped a shelf in my closets! (If you're an organized teacher, I'm so sorry for putting that image in your head.) But in my desperate search, do you know what I found? Every extra bit of math manipulative sets that were once sent along with curriculums we previewed and that we were allowed to keep regardless of whether we purchased the program. All teachers should challenge themselves to scavenge for leftover curriculum materials that students can transform into new learning toys. I'm glad I did, and you'll see why as you read the next section.

MATH MANIPULATIVES

It was one of these long-lost math manipulatives that helped me first recognize a solid academic skill in Elle. She couldn't show me much with pencil and paper or even spoken words during one-on-one assessments. Even when it came to demonstrating a skill as simple as sorting objects into groups using objects of my choosing, she struggled to do so on a worksheet or verbally. However, when the task presented itself in a form she was comfortable with, she did more than expected without even knowing it. I still remember the day I took this picture!

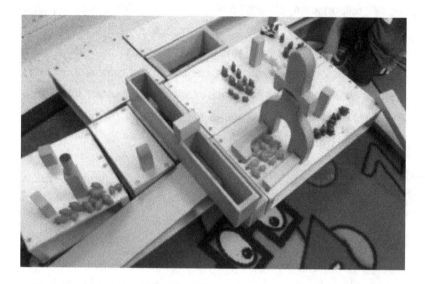

I was walking around our classroom during stations observing and documenting various goals. My students were busy working and playing in different areas with their family groups. This specific observation was made during our math station block, so there was a lot of learning going on covering a range of academic levels. During these stations, students were able to work at their own pace within their group. As usual, there was the have-to activity for all students to complete, and then they had time to play with their can-do activities.

Elle and her group were in the block area on this particular day playing math games on our interactive whiteboard to practice our current math goals. By the time I was walking around, her group had already finished their required activity. As I approached the blocks, I saw Elle working very hard, a determined look on her face as she balanced blocks, set up ramps, and laid out teddy bear counters. I asked her about the structure she was building, and she very excitedly told me she was building houses for different bear families.

"This house is for the green bear family, and this one is for the blue bear family!"

"Wow! That's awesome, Elle, keep it up."

My response was extremely heartfelt but may have come out with a tone of surprise because, until this moment, I had no idea that she knew how to sort objects. I grew even more excited when I looked closer and realized she was sorting the bears by more than one attribute. We hadn't even covered the topic in math yet, and Elle was already doing it perfectly. Take a look back at the picture of her work, and you'll see why I quickly asked her to explain to me why the green bears were lined up that way.

"I sorted the big bears in one line, the medium bears in another, and the little bears in the other one."

Where most people would simply nod their heads in agreement, I celebrated this moment with Elle. I call this a teachable moment, one that turned into a great conversation and lesson. What may seem like a simple task that kids can naturally do was a huge accomplishment for Elle. She was showing me proficiency in an academic standard we hadn't begun to discuss. Her skill had nothing to do with anything I had taught her. And the fact that she didn't realize what she was doing before we discussed it made this moment even better.

This magical story so simply and elegantly proves my point of this whole book. When we allow kids to be kids, the learning happens naturally. The explanations you then give your students will seem obvious to them, and you'll see a desire and love of learning that organically grow. Use these little glimpses of learning as opportunities to encourage and inspire the rest of your students. I asked Elle if she would like to show the rest of the class what she had done and teach them how to sort objects in two different ways. I will never forget the smile on this little girl's face and the excitement in her voice when I let her get up on our stage to teach her friends something *she* knew how to do.

STUFFED ANIMALS

My students loved taking stuffed animals and Beanie Babies from our dramatic play center to create zoo exhibits out of blocks. Fun, right? Their imaginations were soaring, and I was able to witness some amazing social interactions between them all. My students took it upon themselves to get paper, markers, and tape to create signs and maps for their zoo. (What!? On their own?) It was so cool to see the play turn into writing practice and then speaking practice as they began giving zoo tours to me and students from other family groups.

HOT WHEELS AND MATCHBOX CARS

I love bringing my favorite childhood toys into my classroom just as I do with board games and card games. I grew up playing with Hot Wheels and still love playing with them with my own kids. I have a very hard time telling my son no when he wants to take a dollar to the grocery store on shopping trips so he can pick out a new Hot Wheels car. We have quite the extensive collection at home. I also have an extensive collection in my classroom, made up of cars that I've bought, found, and accepted as donations over the years.

My students have used Hot Wheels in multiple educational ways that allowed me to check off, through observation, a bunch of skills they were developing. After some modeling and brainstorming, my students were using the Hot Wheels cars to count, sort, sequence, and more. We made groups of cars sorted by color, type of vehicle, and whether they had numbers. We sequenced cars in order based on the numbers we found on them, too. With basic modeling, you can facilitate play-based learning situations into many areas where students might not do it on their own.

To help keep the learning with Hot Wheels going nonstop, I brought in a couple of drawers for nuts and bolts from a local hardware store and labeled them with uppercase letters, lowercase letters, and numbers. I then took a white correction pen and added letters and numbers to random Hot Wheels cars. Now as the kids were cleaning up after stations, they had to put the cars back in their correct place in our "parking garage." The lowercase-*a* car had to be parked in the uppercase-*A* garage space. The car with five dots on it had to be parked in the number-*5* garage space. What other labels could you add to the vehicles and drawers to recreate this activity?

One of my students working hard to put the cars away in their correct places.

I also used cars to adapt another game that I first learned about from Dr. Jean. I once saw her present about simple ways to play in the classroom, and she showed a game she called parking lot. This game has been adapted by multiple teachers online with different versions and themes, but the main idea behind the game is very simple and the materials are easy to create. Students match Hot Wheels cars to parking spaces on a board or mat, based on a certain skill. In the picture, these students were matching numerals on the cars to a numbered set of dots on spaces in the parking lot.

Teamwork happens naturally when the expectations for family are in place.

RAMPS AND MEASUREMENT

To continue with our love of Hot Wheels, I decided to incorporate the narrow orange plastic tracks into our learning fun in the block area. This idea actually stemmed from my students' interest in learning about the sports they saw on television during the 2018 Winter Olympic Games. During the Olympics that year, the kids were coming to school every day with story after story about what they watched on TV the previous night. I had never seen a group of students so collectively interested in one topic. One of their most favorite sports to talk about was ski jumping. They were amazed at how these athletes flew through the air after launching themselves off the ramp. Another teachable moment was upon me!

During this time, we were also in the middle of our measurement unit, so I decided to combine multiple standards with their love of the Olympics. After some modeling from me, my students were designing, engineering, and testing working ramps. They were also using measuring tapes to track the distance of their ski jumper (Hot Wheels car) and then adjusting the ramp to make their jumper go farther. It was nothing short of awesome to stand back and watch the wheels turn (no pun intended) in their heads. I observed the

students as they were carefully watching the cars travel all the way down the ramps for any time the cars might bounce, shake, or come off the track. When a group spotted the slightest issue with their car's path, they would move and manipulate their blocks and buildings to try to rectify the problem. Never could I have imagined they would be focused and engaged to such an extent!

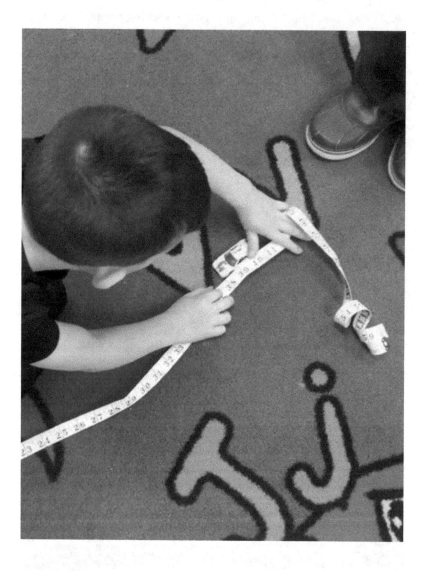

BLUEPRINTS

If you have ever set foot inside a classroom while students are playing in blocks, chances are you've been asked this question: "Can you help me build _____?"

I used to get asked this question all the time. I loved seeing their excitement for building new things, but I wanted to see their creativity shine without my help. I started explaining to them how architects use blueprints to design and build structures. I immediately got another question: "What is an architect, Mr. P?"

After we spent some time researching architects and looking at images of real blueprints, I decided to make some of our own to follow, based on the blocks we had in the classroom. It was extremely simple to do. I took one representative block from each type of block available, tracing them each on white construction paper. I then cut out the shapes and glued them to blue paper in different formations. Some of the formations were basic, house-shaped outlines while others were more complex designs that would challenge my students to build multilevel structures. I created a dozen or so of these one day after school and covered the finished products with a sheet in our block center before my students returned the next day. This was yet another opportunity for me to sell it to them just as I did with the Plinko board. The kids were sold.

They loved laying out blueprints to use as guides for the structures they wanted to build. Soon my students began asking if they could make their own blueprints, and of course I said yes. I repeated the first two steps of my process but didn't glue the white shapes to the blue paper. Instead, I added the shapes and blank blue paper to our block center. My students were now designing and engineering structures on their own!

Teachers loved this idea, too, and started sending me pictures of this activity being used in their own classrooms. These pictures came from my friend Nicole Caggiano, a New Jersey teacher. She was so excited to share these because of the exceptional job her students did when they took this idea and ran with it. Pretty amazing, huh? Awesome work, Nicole!

Take a look around your classroom, through your closets, and even through your garage at home. The simplest items can add a huge amount of learning fun to a block area in your classroom. Fill some tubs with nuts and bolts for fine motor work. Find a bunch of old locks and keys for students to practice sorting and matching. Sometimes just paper and markers can turn the most basic-looking block structures into a 3D model of your hometown or a town from your students' imaginations. When it comes to creative play with hands-on materials, the learning possibilities are endless!

What are some of your favorite activities to add to your blocks center? Share your ideas with me on social media @teacherslearn2.

 ## DISCOVERY TABLE

In both teaching then and on the road presenting now, I have spent a lot of time around kindergarten and early-childhood educators. It's almost always a given that at some point in the conversation the words "when I was in kindergarten" will come up. As soon as someone brings up a memory of the way things used to be, we all start recalling our favorite parts of our childhood classrooms. And just as sure as the conversation turns to our own memories, you can also count on someone using the words "sand table" during said conversation. (OK, I admit that it's usually me.) I loved that thing! I can still remember it was a red table, with a blue drop-in interior, that sat on a wooden stand. It was on the wall opposite of our classroom windows, and it was full of scoops and funnels and had one of those sand spinners that sifted sand from the top of a tower down through multiple spinning wheels. I kind of want to take a trip to my hometown elementary school and play in that sand table with one of those spinners right now!

Over the years, sand tables have taken on new names and have included new items. The buzzwords have changed from *sensory table* to *discovery bin* and every combination of such words in between. Regardless of what you call it, this place should allow students to learn through discovery and play using hands-on activities that encourage children to explore the world around them. I referred to the one in my classroom as a discovery table, so that's what we'll call it in this chapter.

My discovery table comes with a touching background story that I have to share before we get into the activities we did there. It was custom-built by a friend of mine, and it was super fun and super functional! I appreciate so much that it was built by a friend, but I take even greater pleasure in knowing who that friend built it for. My friend Ben built this table for his mother, Honor, my mentor teacher I mentioned in the beginning of this book. Honor passed away in 2013 after retiring from teaching kindergarten, and her son asked me if I would like to have the table for my own classroom. I knew that Honor had put it to great use, and I was honored to carry on the tradition of learning through play that had started in her classroom with the table. My students absolutely loved it, and I treasured having it.

I bet you're wondering what made this table so cool, huh? Well, here it is. The table was an old wooden door with three sections cut into it. Beneath the door a wooden box extended the depth of the three cutouts. Each of these cutout sections was the perfect size to hold a shallow plastic tub. This allowed for incredibly easy use and cleanup when changing out the items I placed in the table. Thanks to Ben's clever design I never had to dump out and sweep up sand, rice, beans, or corn again. All I had to do was take out a tub we had finished using and drop in a different tub with new items in it. Besides holding tubs full of items, it also worked wonders for keeping track of Lite-Brite pegs that would otherwise bounce all over the floor when they rolled off a regular classroom table.

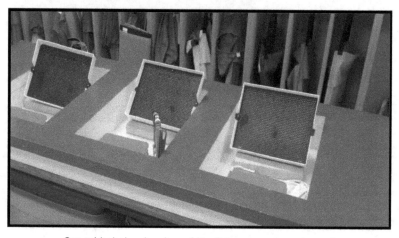

Our table helped us keep Lite-Brite pegs, magnets, and more confined in those bins and off the floor.

Throughout the year, I would change the plastic tubs in the table, and my students would get to play with new and exciting sensory items. As I did with the other areas of my classroom, I tried my best to include fun and engaging educational activities along with the sensory items to truly make this another learn-through-play area.

The list of items and activities that follow helped me blend play and learning seamlessly, all while sticking to the hands-on approach. Let's take a look at some of our favorites.

SHELLED CORN AND SOYBEANS

Living in Illinois and teaching at a school surrounded by fields allowed me easy access to these crops. I'm totally kidding! I did not, I repeat, did not steal crops from the local farmers. Luckily, one of the teachers on my team came from a generous farming family who was willing to donate shelled corn and soybeans to our classrooms anytime we needed it. We used the tubs of corn and beans in the fall as we learned about harvest time and celebrated the farmers of our community during our county's annual corn festival.

To connect with the fall and harvest theme, the activities I added to our table at this time included pictures of apples, pumpkins, cornstalks, leaves, and more. Every fall- or farm-themed memory game I owned that my students had once played on a table or the floor, they now played in the corn and beans! I would bury the memory cards in the tubs so the images couldn't be seen, and the students would take turns pulling out cards to find matches. This simple twist on a classic game helped it become one that my students looked forward to every time we changed tubs, because they knew there would most definitely be a new themed version to play.

Brand-new area, brand-new center, brand-new games, same old philosophy! If I could change the content in our discovery table without changing the rules for new games, it made my job that much easier. Throughout the fall season, I replaced the corn and beans with twigs, leaves, acorns, and other items that fit with our seasonal activities. The ease of engaging students with everyday items never ceased to amaze me. Adding in some magnifying glasses and a microscope allowed my students to explore crops, their root systems, and all the other parts of the plants. We had always done cut-and-glue activities to learn the plant parts, but seeing them up close and in real life made for a much more meaningful learning experience. This research also led to my students' drawing and labeling pictures of plants, which might not have happened otherwise. The most satisfying part of all was that their scientific exploration of the items in the table, and of other items you'll read about in the rest of this section, prompted questions of me that naturally created more teachable moments.

COLORED AND SCENTED RICE

Remember that you can use everyday items to create instant engagement, even though these same items typically wouldn't get children to turn their heads. One of these items is rice. Basic, everyday white rice from the dollar store. I had seen multiple teachers posting pictures on social media of dyed rice. The images attracted my attention immediately. Teachers were using rice for sensory bins, seek-and-find bottles, crafts, and more. I knew that my students would flock to these tubs of colored rice just like the corn and soybeans, no matter what activity I threw in it, so I looked up a recipe and got to work.

Because winter was the first season I introduced the dyed rice to my students, I wanted the rice itself to reflect that. I dyed one bag of rice using red food coloring and left a second bag white. I mixed the red and white rice together into one tub to create the perfect wintery mix. Think peppermints and candy canes! To enhance the sensory experience even more, I took a lesson from my buddy Greg Smedley-Warren from the Kindergarten Smorgasboard and I added peppermint oil to the rice. We had a new discovery tub that looked, felt, and smelled fun! My students were beyond excited to dive in and play games in this new addition to our classroom.

This first introduction of rice to the classroom happened to occur around the time that I was introducing my students to measurement, so it was the perfect time to add funnels, scoops, and beakers to the discovery table. OK, take a second and put yourself in the shoes of a five-year-old, really. Turn on the young-child mindset, and try to tell me you wouldn't flip when your teacher removed the lids of the discovery tubs and you saw multiple sizes of jars and beakers, shiny red funnels, and all different kinds of scoops. Admit it, you would be thrilled! My students were, too.

In addition to being gifted with Honor's discovery table, I was happy to inherit a ton of my friend's other classroom stuff as well when she retired. One of my favorite items was her set of various-sized beakers, jars, and containers that she had collected over the years. I know it doesn't sound like anything special, but the set included some cool, odd-shaped, vintage-looking beakers. If you ever come across these types of items, hang on to them for your classroom. It may also be beneficial to reach out to high school science teachers and parents who work in the science industry, or even to search for random flower vases that would work just as well as beakers.

Honor had labeled each container with a letter and created a recording page with the matching letters on them. The task for my students was to estimate how many scoops of rice each container could hold, and then use a specified scoop to measure and check their estimations. The recording sheet had pictures of the containers and two boxes next to each picture. One box was for the estimation, and one box was for the actual measurement of how much the container could hold. My favorite type of learning activity was taking place each time my students visited this station—they were learning, and they didn't even realize it. They were practicing estimation skills, measurement skills, and number writing in ways that engaged them. Add the fact that they were actively doing this around a table and enjoying themselves, and we were hitting every part of the definition of play! To add to the learning experience, each family group compared the estimations they made with those of the other groups. This in turn led to a whole-class discussion on estimation, measurement, and comparing.

SHREDDED PAPER AND RUBBER WORMS

Yep, rubber worms. This activity was another genius design from my good friend Honor. During our rainy spring season in Illinois, there is never a shortage of worms wiggling their way across the sidewalks. Kids are fascinated by these creatures and the overwhelming number of them that emerge from the saturated ground. To ensure that no worms were harmed in the making of this activity, we decided to create some fun activities using rubber worms instead. Once again, the best part was that the kids' imagination took over, and they loved it!

First, I asked for donations and bought as many rubber worms as I could. I tried to get worms in multiple sizes and colors so they could be used for various activities. To create dirt for our new class pets, I shredded black and brown construction paper using a regular paper shredder to make long, thin strips. I filled a couple of the plastic tubs that fit my discovery table with the newly mixed soil for our worms to hide in. Here are some of the activities that ensued:

- **Sorting:** Rubber worms come in multiple colors and shapes. Some have different textures, and some even have different ends on them. It helps if you can collect many different styles for sorting activities. Now dig out any type of sorting mat or tray you own, and you've got stations that can last quite a while with your students. I love using various sizes of muffin trays for activities like this because it leaves the sorting decisions up to the students themselves and doesn't limit the number of different ways they can sort one type of object. I always make a point to challenge my students to sort by as many attributes as possible. With this activity, I've seen groups of worms spread across the tables, including green worms, brown worms, speckled worms, short worms, broken worms, and more. When you allow your students to think independently, you'll be so proud of the solutions they come up with on their own.

- **Length comparison:** Rubber worms are easy to cut apart, so why not create some different sizes to use as a measurement tool? I cut worms into various lengths, and then my students would pull out three worms at a time to order from longest to shortest, and vice versa.
- **Counting:** Students set a timer and pulled out as many worms as possible using plastic tweezers before the timer counted down to zero. After the timer went off, each student counted their own pile of worms to see how many they collected. This counting led to comparing numbers by greater than/ less than as well.
- **Letters:** I added laminated letter mats to the area. Students would collect worms and lay them onto the mats to form letters. There was instant engagement with this basic letter recognition and letter formation activity. I also added laminated sight-word mats to this area for my students to form sight words with the worms they pulled from the tubs.

SAND AND SEASHELLS

Ah, the classic sensory item—sand! What kid doesn't love playing in the sand? OK, OK, it's time to put your own sensory problems aside of not being able to stand a mess and not wanting to sweep up sand from the floor, and remember that it's all about the kids!

The activities mentioned previously in this chapter can all be carried over to use in the sand table. Memory games, measurement activities, and sorting activities can all be done by adding items to the sand table. One logical item to introduce in the sand is seashells. I have gallon-sized zipper storage bags full of seashells that have been collected and given to me from various people over the years. Kids are fascinated by seashells and love getting their hands on them.

These are a few different ways I've made seashells work in the classroom for learning activities.

- **Sorting:** Students used sand sifters, shovels, and brushes to collect seashells from the sand and sort them on trays. By the time this activity was introduced to my students, they had already been through our sorting units in math and had a firm grasp on different sorting rules. As a result, I didn't give many directions on how they were to sort the shells. I let them create the sorting rules on their own with their friends. As they pulled seashells from the sand, I've observed my students sorting by color, size, shape, texture, and more. They also created sorting rules for two attributes.
- **Classifying:** With a simple online search on seashell classification, you can find images that will tell you the specific names of different types of seashells. I printed out a few of these labeled images, laminated them, and stuck them in the station tub for that area. My students took their love of seashells to a whole new level, and before I knew it, they were teaching me all about seashells!
- **Memory:** My students had been playing classic memory games quite a bit by the time I introduced this game. I went through my bunches of seashells and pulled out ones that had a wide space on the inside and were light enough to write on with a permanent marker. I wrote duplicates of sight words from our list on the inside of the shells and lined them up in the sand in multiple rows—instant twist on memory!

You can create similar activities by adding letters, numbers, math problems, and more to the shells. Think like a teacher, and I'm sure you'll come up with many more.

WATER

Adding water to the discovery table can send the same shiver of fear through a teacher's spine that sand does. Don't let the fear of wet floors and shoes steer you away from letting your students explore and learn in a water table. There are plenty of toy boats and ocean creatures at dollar stores during the summer months, and the simple addition of these items will bring a child's imagination to life! You can also create activities simply by adding manipulatives from around your classroom to the water table.

- **Teddy bear boats:** I brought in some aluminum foil, showed my students how to form squares of foil into boats, added our bucket of teddy bear counters to the station, and we had a fun new estimation and counting activity. My students formed their boats, estimated how many teddy bears could fit before they sank, then started counting using one-to-one correspondence. Math standards—check!

- **Sink and float:** I know this seems like an obvious one, but I learned something new the last time I did a sink-and-float unit in my classroom. Instead of keeping our tub dropped into the discovery table, I pulled it out and set it on top of the table. This allowed my students to look through the sides of the tub to see from an underwater point of view if the items were actually floating. Allow your students to use items from around the classroom for this, too. When they have choice in what they get to experiment with, the learning goes to a new level. You can almost see their thought processes engage.

To do any of these table activities, you don't need a giant table like the one I was lucky enough to inherit. Actually, you don't need a table at all. Pick up some plastic tubs, gather some of the items mentioned in this chapter, and let your kids be kids. Your students will love seeing a tub full of new hands-on items from time to time in your classroom. And don't let the items I've mentioned limit you, either. What would you add to a sensory table or tub? Answer that question out loud and put it into action!

4
PLAY ON THE CHEAP!

CHEAP PLAY doesn't just mean finding items for low prices; it also means using the resources at your disposal to create new and engaging learning opportunities for your students. I've obviously tried to save myself money any chance I could, but my inspiration for creating cheap activities started way before I became a teacher. I grew up in a wonderful, loving household with parents who made sure we had everything we needed. I was also lucky to have some pretty amazing toys and games. But my parents were not the type to spend money on toys just because we asked. (I'm thankful for that now.) Though I might not have agreed with those decisions when I was younger, my parents inadvertently encouraged more creativity in my siblings and me. My brother and I created awesome Hot Wheels racetracks by drawing on large pieces of cardboard. Shoe boxes and other boxes of various sizes made great buildings and ramps. We created our own fun outside all the time by using the natural elements around us, too. This chapter is dedicated to the frugal voice inside of us all. Cheap play doesn't mean discounted learning or cutting corners to reach a goal. Play on the cheap can actually encourage more creativity in your students, and you!

NEXT GENERATION STUDENT SCIENTISTS

"Like learning to count, or to read, learning how to 'do' science is a lifelong process." This quote is by Peggy Ashbrook, early childhood science teacher. I love that this quote was said by an early childhood teacher that believes in the importance of doing. Far too often we see science curriculums centered around textbooks and worksheets with an occasional experiment thrown in here and there. At the upper-grade levels, I understand that this type of research and reading plays an important part in the learning process. But at the kindergarten and primary levels, most of the learning taking place is centered around understanding the scientific process, and I don't believe there is any better way to teach that process than by doing science.

Science is one of my favorite subjects to teach. The way students look on in eager anticipation of a miracle about to happen before their very eyes is a moment I lived for when I was in the classroom. It wasn't always that way though. At the beginning of my teaching career, I was doing what I thought I had to do by following the science manual our school had given me. And, in all honesty, I wasn't reaching the excitement levels that I'd hoped I would, but who could blame my students when the material I was using was nothing more than worksheets and a few simple experiments?

I knew I had to find a way to make science as exciting for my students to learn as it was for me to teach. I started looking through teacher catalogs and found some interesting units, materials for science experiments, and tools to learn about the world around us. The toughest part about carrying out my plan for these items was that these things were very expensive. I didn't have the budget, but

I did have the motivation and desire to do more for my students. So I adapted a teaching technique from my friend Kim Adsit, and science quickly took the engagement in my classroom to heights never known.

Beginning with making all my students feel like real scientists, here's how it works!

CHEAP SCIENTIST GEAR

1. I started by taking pictures of my students and myself on the very first day of school. I always do this anyway, so I told my students these were the regular old first-day-of-school pictures. The key here is making sure you get a picture of yourself!

2. After getting a headshot for everyone in the class, I took the pictures and dropped them in a Google Slides document. I also added some fun clip art and text. I printed these cards out, laminated them, and added a safety pin to the back of each card to create name badges.

3. Next, I made a trip to a local store to pick up size small, men's V-neck T-shirts from the clearance section. Using a permanent marker, I drew some simple lines on the shirts and added a pocket and some buttons, creating lab coats for all my students.

4. I added the name badges to the lab coats, collected some safety goggles from a parent donation, slapped a label on the side of a cardboard box, and put all the items inside the box. The plan of surprise was in place. I dropped the box off with the school secretary and asked her to deliver it to me in my classroom at a specific time.

5. Sell it! I got a knock on our classroom door later that afternoon. Our secretary told me the mail had just been delivered, including a box for me and my students. I thanked her with exaggerated emotion, trying to show as much surprise in my voice as possible. Then my students and I quickly dug into the box!

The first item we pulled out was this letter addressed to my students and me. (Remember the selling factor grows when they don't think it came from you.)

Dr. Science
Dr. Science laboratories
123 Laboratory Way
Scienceville, USA

To _____

Hey Kids! My name is Dr. Science, and I LOVE science experiments! I'm so busy at my laboratory that I'm in need of some help from you! I have too many experiments to finish on my own. I've included one of my experiments in this box for you. Can you help? I will send you a new experiment each week along with everything you'll need to complete it. All I ask is that you follow the steps of the Scientific Process, and that you keep track of all of the data that you collect. I'm so thankful for your help, and I can't wait to see what you discover through these experiments. You are all now official Dr. Science Professors! Work hard and have fun!

Dr. Science

This letter can be found in the unit Kim and I wrote titled
The Science Box, available on Teachers Pay Teachers.

After we read the letter addressed to us from my imaginary friend Dr. Science, we pulled out all the materials I listed in the steps above as well as the items for our first science experiment. This picture shows the exact effect I was hoping for, and thanks to Dr. Science, I got it!

Each week, Dr. Science would send a new box with a new experiment inside. Each delivery brought the same level of reactions from the students. The arrival of the boxes made for some of the most exciting times in our classroom. Not once did my students question the process of how the box kept showing up each week. Nor did they ever question the fact that some of the materials inside the box on certain weeks were items from our very classroom, that had my name written on them, that they had actually played with before. That's just more proof of the power of selling it when introducing new things. While I don't have enough time—or enough pages in this book—to share every single experiment our class did, here are a couple of the favorites.

APPLE DROP SCIENCE

Each year, our kindergarten program does a huge unit on apples. We read books, do crafts, learn how apples grow, have apples as snacks, and tie as much of our curriculum as we can to apples. During this unit, the students all bring apples from home for graphing and snacking, and it never fails that at some point an apple will get bruised. One of my students innocently asked how apples get bruised and why they sometimes turn brown. Those very questions are what prompted me

to start the Dr. Science boxes. It was the perfect opportunity to introduce the scientific process to my eager young learners. In most cases with primary science teaching, understanding the scientific process is really the objective anyway, so I turned that innocent question into a lesson. Along with our first experiment, Dr. Science also included posters for our classroom listing the steps of the scientific process.

We had apples in our classroom, and we had already been making observations. We also had the question that had been asked by my curious young student. Next came our task of making a hypothesis. To keep my philosophy of learning through play alive, I wanted to conduct this experiment with as much engagement, activity, and enjoyment as possible, so I decided to take it to the extreme. Dr. Science challenged my students to make a hypothesis based on the following statements:

- If my teacher drops an apple on the floor, I think this will happen.
- If my teacher drops an apple from a ladder, I think this will happen.
- If my teacher drops an apple from the school's roof, I think this will happen.

I'm sure you can imagine the excitement my students showed when that last statement was read to them. One little girl in my class immediately shouted, "NO!" Well, little did they know that everything was in place for us to conduct these three steps that very day. Again, not one question of how or why a ladder was in our classroom or why our custodian was already available to drop items from the roof. Sell it! I'm not going to lie, this experiment was pretty darn awesome! If you want to see the reactions for yourself, you can see it on my YouTube channel with this link.

Apple Drop
Science Video

After the kids and I put on our scientific gear, otherwise known as PPE (personal protective equipment), we all grabbed our clipboards and the recording pages that Dr. Science had included in the box. The students' recording pages offered them spaces for drawing and writing a hypothesis for each of the three questions. We discussed the importance of making hypotheses based on what we already knew about apples and what we had observed if any had been dropped throughout the week during our other activities. Then we got busy conducting our experiments.

It was nothing short of magical to watch the different reactions of my students as the apples fell from different heights. But nothing could have prepared me for their excitement as our custodian chucked three apples off the roof of our gymnasium onto the asphalt below. That excitement alone was enough to make this experiment amazing, but the eagerness of every single one of my students to discuss, report, and record the results made it even better. Never before had I seen so many kids so anxious to check and compare their hypotheses to the findings of the experiment. And this was just the first box of many from Dr. Science.

PULL-A-SKATER

Remember in the last chapter how I mentioned my students were slightly obsessed with the Winter Olympic Games? Well, that wasn't a one-and-done activity. How could it be? How could I show a shared interest once and then let it go? I couldn't, can't, and never will! I decided to let Dr. Science in on all the fun of our Olympics study. The question posed this time still related to forces and interactions but focused more on pushes and pulls. Like the scene that started off our week of apple drop science, at about one o'clock on a Friday afternoon we heard two knocks on our door, followed by "Mr. Peterson, this package was just dropped off for you in the office." This time there were no questions or looks of wonder on the faces of my students. There were only screams of elation: "Dr. Science was here!"

The box delivered to us this week was once again full of simple items, most of which were from around our very own classroom, and directions from Dr. Science. Inside, the students and I found paper plates, pipe cleaners, paper clips, and magnet wands. The directions were as follows:

1. Bend a pipe cleaner into the shape of a figure skater and glue it to a paper clip. We had been reading about figure skaters as well as watching Olympic clips, so my students created skaters in many different positions.

 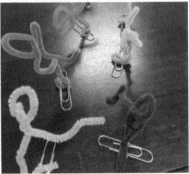

2. Each student got a paper plate to act as their ice skating rink. Using what they had learned previously about magnets, the students tried to push and pull their figure skaters around on the ice.

3. To encourage more exploration with pushes and pulls, we created ice skating routines for the figure skaters to follow. My students really had to focus on the type of movement and pressure they would apply to their magnet to keep their skater on the routine path.

Now, I know there is nothing in the Next Generation Science Standards (NGSS) that tells me to drop apples from different heights or create magnetic figure skaters and Olympic routines, but there are standards that focus on forces, interactions, and the effect different forces can have on one object when it interacts with another object. These two experiments are prime examples of the philosophy I introduced earlier: "It's not about what you teach but how you teach it that makes all the difference."

If you'd like to see more experiments related to Dr. Science and his science box, you can find them in a unit I created with my friend Kim Adsit.

Get your own copy
of *The Science
Box* here.

THE DOLLAR STORE TEACHER CHALLENGE

I saw an electronic card recently that made me literally laugh out loud until I remembered how true it can be. It read, "Here's hoping all the teachers made enough money at their summer jobs to afford school supplies for this school year!"

Sad, but true. We all know, all too well, that there is a serious budget issue affecting schools nationwide. Teacher layoffs, program cuts, and overcrowded classrooms cause stress on the administrators and teachers in school buildings. Teachers are constantly being asked to do more but are given little to none of the supplies required to meet the needs of their students. I'll be the first to admit that a classroom isn't about the stuff inside of it. It's about the students and the teacher. But those students and teachers need that stuff to enhance their educational experience, and a larger variety of items readily available to a teacher can help reach more students of varying academic levels and interests.

With a lot of creativity and a bit of exploring while strolling up and down different aisles, teachers can find a bunch of items for classroom engagement at bargain stores or the many dollar stores across the country. A lot of times, the seasonal items in these stores are premade games, making it easy to grab some fun additions that won't break the bank. However, while the easy route can be a great one, I love a good challenge as well! It was in this need for a challenge that my YouTube series *The Dollar Store Teacher Challenge* was created.

My goal with each of the videos in this series is to try to bypass the teacher section at my local dollar stores and find items elsewhere. I go to the store with no specific plan in mind other than keeping my eyes open and searching until an item sparks my interest. I try my hardest to find things not typically thought of as classroom items and turn them into a game or activity to be used in a classroom.

I had no idea when I started this challenge how many episodes I would do, and though I've taken breaks from time to time, I quickly realized there is always something to be discovered in the aisles of these stores. After sharing the first few videos on my channel and telling teachers about it at conference sessions, a whole new challenge came my way. I soon had teachers from all over the world messaging me with their own challenges to create activities of their choosing. Here's an example: "Adam, I challenge you to make a game using a makeup mirror, small paper cups, and toothpicks."

Really, that was one of the challenges I received. I try to reply as promptly as possible with two simple words: challenge accepted! Every time I begin a new challenge, whether it is my own idea or one sent to me by someone else, I always follow these two rules:

1. If possible, refrain from purchasing all items from the teacher section. If needed, the challenge can include dice, spinners, or similar teacher tools, but no challenge can be a premade classroom activity in itself.

2. Try to keep the cost of the activity under five dollars total. If the activity created will be used by small groups of students, it may require purchasing multiples of each item, but the main components of one set of the game should not exceed five dollars.

Are you ready to try? Will you accept the challenge?
Ready, set, shop!

To help spark some of your own creative thinking, I have included some of my favorite activities created following the rules above. Please be aware that these items might not be available at all dollar-store locations. Plus, some are seasonal items, so you may have to search around a bit to find similar things.

SEEK-AND-FIND CANS

Here's what you need:

- 1 bag of white rice
- 1 bag of letter beads (or beads of choice)
- 3 small metal containers

The metal containers we used for this activity can be found in the office supply section and are meant for storing things like paperclips, staples, thumbtacks, and other small items. They have a snap-on lid with a clear plastic insert that allows your students to see what's inside. Creating this engaging activity is as simple as opening the container, filling it halfway with rice, and adding beads of your choice. Once you have the container filled with the beads you want, put on the lid and keep it on with hot glue or tape. Once the container is sealed, give it a good shake and, voila! Your students can shake up the cans, peer through the lid, and name the items they see hiding in the rice. You now have a seek-and-find game that can be used to meet a variety of standards, depending on the type of beads or other items you put inside the container.

When I used alphabet beads in the containers, I added one bead with each letter of the alphabet. The task was finding, matching, and crossing off letters on a marker board until all the letters were found. I've also strategically added letter beads that would form certain high-frequency words, creating a homemade version of the ever-popular game Boggle.

If you have students working on color identification or matching, just add multicolored beads. If you want to work on number identification or simple math problems, add number beads of your choice. The possibilities for this activity are many, depending on the types of beads you can find. However, don't let the beads limit your creativity.

In the episode of my video series where I re-created this activity, I couldn't find letter beads at my local dollar store. I knew I could somehow adapt that part of the supplies, and I was able to when I found a whole section of puffy plastic alphabet stickers. Problem solved! I just bought a few packs of stickers and stuck them together, back to back. Doing this allowed me to place the stickers in the rice without the rice sticking to their backs.

COTTON SWABS AND DOG BOWLS

"What?"

Did you just say that out loud?

I get it, it's OK. Teachers say that to me all the time when I tell them I created games using items found in the pet-supply aisle. Don't limit your creativity to predictable items and sections of the store. I kept this principle in mind when I was searching for a fun Halloween-themed item for my students. I had already placed a package of cotton swabs in my cart, knowing they could easily be used as skeleton bones for a craft. Many different variations of skeleton bone crafts use cotton swabs glued to black construction paper, and I had done a few of them before. This challenge wasn't about re-creating a craft though, so I passed up the paper and glue and turned the corner into the pet supplies. My eyes immediately caught sight of a dog food dish decorated with white bones all around the sides! I knew I could create an activity that had my students reaching into the bowl to pull out and count skeleton bones.

That wasn't enough for me, though, because I didn't want them simply to use their hands to pull out the cotton swabs. I headed to the seasonal items and found exactly what I needed to put the final touch on this activity. Hanging on an endcap at my eye level, begging me to buy them, were salad tongs in the shape of skeleton arms and hands. The teacher gods were on my side that day for sure! I quickly threw the skeleton tongs in my cart and headed to the checkout, spending a total of only three dollars.

Since this game was going to be played during station time, I needed only one set to accomplish the goal I had in mind. The idea I had was to incorporate this activity into the rotation of my math stations as a game to review counting and tally marks. I created a simple recording sheet to go along with the game, which my students could use to show me their progress.

Students took turns using the skeleton tongs to grab the cotton swab bones from the bowl. With their haul laid on the table, they worked together to organize the bones into groups of five in tally mark formations. They then drew tally marks in the large box on their recording sheet to match the amount created with the bones. Using skip counting, the students worked together to count the total amount of bones collected and record that number in the small box on their recording sheet. When all the students were finished recording the information for that round, the bones went back in the bowl and the next student took a turn. Simple, cheap, and best of all, engaging!

One would think that such a task would not hold the attention of a five-year-old child for long, but that assumption was proven wrong the first time I introduced this game to my students. The recording sheet I created had space to record only three different turns, with room on the back to do more if they wanted to. The task took only a short portion of time to complete at that station area. After turning in their papers, my students were free to play with other items in the area, but to my amazement, they returned to the station and continued the skeleton tally activity for no other purpose than fun. When children are learning in a way that's new and enjoyable, the learning never stops. My students played this game over and over, and we eventually came up with other ways to use these items throughout the rest of the school year.

The bonus of using a platform such as YouTube to share content with teachers is the amount of networking I can accomplish with the simple click of a button. Besides getting challenges from teachers, I also got some phenomenal suggestions for cotton swab/dog bowl variations as soon as I published a video about the activity to YouTube. The wealth of knowledge that can be shared when like-minded people start connecting with one another is outstanding! Here are a couple of great ideas from other creative educators.

- **Colors:** One fabulous follower taught me something new when she suggested using colored cotton swabs. The idea was simple but something I had never heard of before. Instead of buying the everyday white cotton swabs, you can purchase ones that have a colored stick. How had I never heard of these? Using the same materials, we have thrown yet another variation into the mix for different learners. Students can take turns pulling colored cotton swabs out of the dog bowl to sort by color.

- **Measurement:** This idea is a great way to add a fun twist to measuring and comparing length. Students use the tongs to pull out a bunch of cotton swabs and then lay them down end to end. Using a tape measure or other length-measuring tool, students can measure and record the length of the cotton swab train they have built. My students took this to a whole new level on their own when they started seeing how many cotton swabs it took to measure their bodies as they took turns lying on the floor.

- **Letters:** Why limit this cheap find to one subject area? Cotton swabs can serve many purposes and be used over and over again, if you think across curriculums. One YouTube sub-scriber suggested using them to form letters rather than tally mark formations. Brilliant! Instead of counting the number of cotton swabs pulled from the bowl, your students can try to form as many letters as possible by laying the cotton swabs out in various formations. Don't stop there though! What about taking all those letters you just formed and creating students' names or sight words?

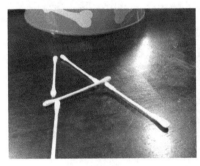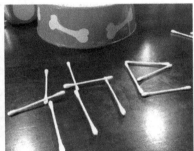

AQUARIUM ROCKS AND DECORATIVE STONES

As you've learned by now, I am a big believer in using manipulatives in place of worksheets to create hands-on learning experiences for children. That belief especially holds true when it comes to recogniz-ing and ordering numbers or letters of the alphabet. If the focus for the child is simple recognition and ordering, provide tactile items to do so instead of having him or her copy and write letters or numbers on a worksheet. The process of tracing and copying letters and num-bers can help a child who is ready to start writing, but not all chil-dren are ready at the same time. For those still learning what a letter is and how to recognize and order it, the process of then writing that letter can be frustrating and difficult.

We have all had our fair share of manipulatives in the shapes of letters and numbers. My kids loved the magnetic ones and could often be found spelling names, building sentences, or putting numbers in order to the highest number they possibly could. To keep this love of learning alive and add a new twist, I found something that would accomplish the same goal.

I was walking through the aisles of yet another dollar store one day and came across bags of decorative stones. I refer to them as aquarium rocks because they were what we used to decorate the giant aquarium at our house. I remembered seeing an idea for these rocks online somewhere and knew I could implement them into my classroom immediately. The idea was to use a permanent marker to write letters and numbers on the individual rocks. How easy is that? I bought a few bags to make sure I had enough to create multiple sets, picked up a fresh black permanent marker, and headed home to label some rocks.

- **ABC ordering:** I made two sets of alphabet rocks, one labeled with uppercase letters and the other with lowercase. Now instead of writing the alphabet in order on paper or with magnetic letters, my students were using these bright-colored stones to lay the alphabet out in order. We also added these rocks to our sand table to create another form of memory. Besides ordering letters, my students also practiced matching uppercase letters to lowercase letters.
- **Names:** One of the things I kept in my room was a framed class list that had my students' names and faces on it. I originally created this for my parent volunteers or subs for easily matching names to faces. Once I brought the stones into the room, I had a brand-new use for this photo frame. I set it out on a station table with a basket of stones in front of it. My students found the faces of their friends, read their names, and then spelled their names with the stones. They were so

excited to be able to spell the names of their classmates, and this quickly became a favorite center to visit whenever they had the chance!

- **Numbers:** We used stones labeled with numbers to practice ordering, matching numerals, number combinations, and for practicing counting using one-to-one correspondence. Adding dice, spinners, playing cards, and other number-related items to the aquarium rocks gave my students even more opportunities to practice math skills through play.

- **Sight words:** I purchased extra sets of rocks for this activity because I needed enough to write words on some and letters on others. I created one set of rocks with our sight words written on them. I then created a second set of rocks with letters that spelled out the sight words. My students would pull a sight-word rock from a basket, then use the letter rocks to form that sight word.

STEM CREATIONS

Thanks to the craft section at Dollar Tree, I have created a few different STEM activities that my students have loved and used time and time again to redesign and experiment with creations. If you take a look back and forth from the craft section to the toy section, it's easy to find items that can be used in conjunction with each other to create problem-solving projects that will have your students thinking creatively! An added bonus of the next three examples is that they are all great opportunities to review the scientific process with your students.

- **Toy soldier bridges:** When Disney released *Toy Story 4* in the summer of 2019, I had already begun my *Dollar Store Teacher Challenge* series. I wanted to come up with an idea that somehow related to the movie because kids would love it. I chose the character of the toy soldier to create this activity because you can find toy soldiers in the toy aisle of dollar stores. I also found craft dough, popsicle sticks, and clothespins to add to this activity for cheap. I used the popsicle sticks, craft dough, and clothespins to construct a bridge. I then loaded the bridge with toy soldiers to see how many it could hold. To address the addition of the domain Engineering Design to the national science standards, this activity will no doubt have your students thinking like engineers and adapting their designs to solving problems. You can learn more about this project on my YouTube channel with this QR code.

Watch the bridge-making in action!

- **Marshmallow towers:** Head to Dollar Tree and pick up some toothpicks and marshmallows. What can't you do with these two items! My students have used them to build basic shapes, letters, numbers, and 3D shapes. The real fun, however, started when I posed the following challenge: which group could build the tallest freestanding structure using only marshmallows and toothpicks? They got really creative with this, and the varying ideas really showcased their individual ways of thinking.

- **Sun shades:** One of the Next Generation Science Standards calls for the use of tools and materials to design and build a structure that will reduce the warming effect of sunlight on an area. When I first read that standard, I was a bit shocked and really curious as to how I could make this work with my kindergarten students. With a quick trip to Dollar Tree one evening, I found a few basic materials that helped me meet the standard easily! The first idea that came to mind was to have the students build some type of umbrella. I picked up craft dough, straws, pipe cleaners, and coffee filters and challenged my students to address the standard. With a little direction from me, I was amazed at how they began designing and engineering structures to block out the light from flashlights that they held above their structures. I do this activity with teachers in presentations, and it's always amazing to see the differences among everyone's ideas. (And some people get really creative with the pipe cleaners!)

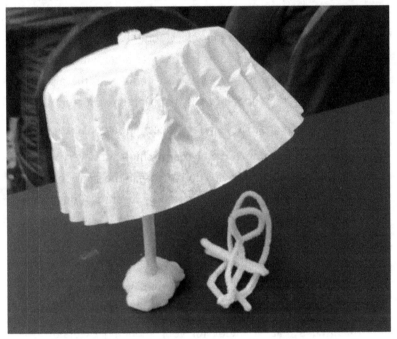

Extra pipe cleaners make for a great sunbather under the umbrella.

The ideas I've shared so far in this chapter are just the bare minimum of what can be created using items from dollar stores. While I consider myself a pretty creative person, I couldn't write this chapter without including the wisdom of my friend Kim Adsit, the self-declared "Dollar Store Diva"!

INSPIRATION FROM THE AISLES

USING PLAY THE DOLLAR STORE DIVA WAY!

Teachers spend money on their classrooms, and lots of it! But every teacher is also looking for a good deal. While there are many school-supply stores, they are often pricey and not local for most teachers. This requires teachers to look for other sources to equip, furnish, and enhance our classroom environments. With a little imagination and just a few bucks, I was able to motivate and engage my students in new ways with items from the aisles of dollar stores. And the good news is that it's pretty simple!

There are a few things to remember in becoming a dollar store diva:

- **Go often.** Dollar stores receive new shipments every week. I was lucky enough to have a dollar store in the same shopping center as my weekly Weight Watchers meeting. A quick pass through the store was all I needed to see if any new items caught my eye. You might also want to consider visiting a few stores. I have found that the same store chain can have different items at their various locations.

- **Go with a friend.** Yes, go with a friend, but not just any friend. Meeting a teacher buddy for your shopping excursion can increase the potential for creativity. It is easy to build an OK idea into a great idea when teachers talk with each other. This collaboration will also enable you to divide and conquer when you discover a few new ideas you want to create. It is quicker to make two copies of the same item than one copy of two different items. If each teacher makes two of one item, they can then swap so they each have two different props!

- **Walk every aisle.** Get out of the teacher aisle. While the items in this section can be helpful, it is not where you are going to find the most engaging resources. The kitchen section, holiday section, and even the greeting cards and gift bags section can offer some great items.

In the following pages, I share with you some of my favorite finds from aisles other than the teacher aisle.

Be sure and check out the aisles for housewares. These scrub brushes make great ducks simply by adding wiggle eyes and a felt oval for the beak. "Five Little Ducks" is a favorite song and rhyme of many teachers. You can easily teach subtraction, one less, or number combinations as the kids use these puppets to role-play as you sing the song.

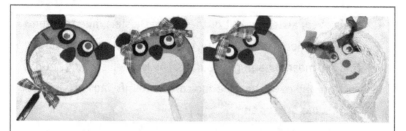

Do you know what these are? Many people I ask don't! They are splatter guards intended to be placed over a skillet to avoid grease splatters. But I think they make great puppets. Simply using spray paint, felt, ribbon, and wiggle eyes, I have created a set of puppets to retell "Goldilocks and the Three Bears."

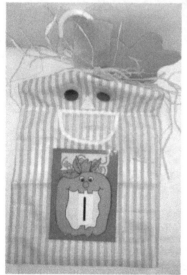

Here's another item from the housewares section that you may not recognize. These are clothespin bags—for hanging on the clothesline to hold the pins. To make these jack-o-lanterns, I added some wiggle eyes, felt stems and leaves, and a little raffia for extra fun. I used Velcro to add the number pumpkins (they sell off-brand hook-and-loop fastener dots at the dollar store), collected a bunch of small toys, and invited my students to clap the number of syllables in each toy name. Then, they fed the toy to the correct pumpkin. Easily change this to a beginning sound game by placing letter cards instead of numerals.

Many cheap ideas can be found on the aisles dedicated to bath supplies, too. These bath toys are a fun, engaging way to sing "Five Speckled Frogs." Simply attach the frogs to clothespins and clip them to a twig. My favorite glue to use is E6000. It holds anything!

Another favorite from the bath supplies … bath mitts! These mitts work equally well for "Five Little Ducks." Not only do these songs offer a brain-friendly way to teach number concepts but repeated singing of songs also develops fluency.

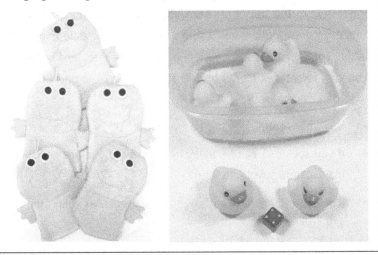

I also found these rubber ducks. When you add water to an activity, the kids love it! For this fun game, the kids roll the dice to see how many ducks to put in the water. Try rolling two dice and add the numbers together. Now put the number of ducks in the pond to represent the sum. What other ways could you use this fun math center?

Move on over to the stationery aisle, where you can find more ideas. Party invitations and thank-you notes usually come in packs of eight to ten cards. For these baby invitations, I simply cut off the front of the cards and added some plastic baby pins from the party section of the store. This makes a fun counting, addition, or subtraction game.

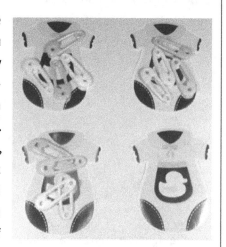

Right next to the stationery aisle, you will find the party supplies. Gift bags are a gold mine! I found these fun cupcake bags and added some candles for a variety of number games. For instance, you can ask your students to do some birthday-themed thinking with these questions:

- How many candles will go on your cake this year?

- If you took one candle away from how old you are now, how many candles would be left?

- If you and your friend add your candles together, what number will you get?

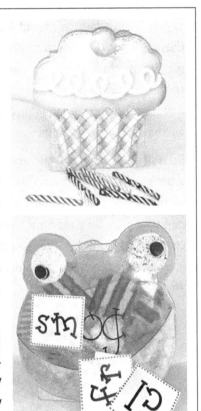

By posing questions like these, you are putting the learning in the hands and minds of your students, with just a simple twist on essential standards and skills.

I also found these delightful frog bags. I made a set of onsets for _og, added a Velcro dot to each card, and wrote __og on the bag. After placing all the onsets inside the bag, I invited the kids to pull one out and stick it to the Velcro to make a new word.

These divided plates are a fun substitute for traditional number bonds. The pirate only needs coins (found in the party section of the store) to provide a motivating way for kids to develop number sense through manipulating the coins to make part/part/whole. By encouraging the use of speaking and listening skills, your students will be

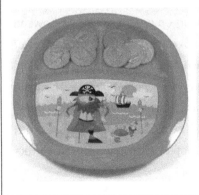

saying, "I used four coins and four coins to make eight coins!" If they say it with a pirate accent, the activity will be much more fun, too. The monster plate and some wiggle eyes (found in the craft section of the store) are another opportunity for kids to develop that conceptual understanding of numbers in an engaging way that will have all your students wanting to practice again and again.

Be sure and check out the seasonal items. These fall leaves make a perfect ABC game along with a few rakes I found in the toy section. I invited the kiddos to rake the leaves. Once they had a pile of leaves, they read each of them. But wait! You can easily change this game by what you choose to write on the leaves. If you want to teach sight words, numerals, shapes, or just about anything, you can!

This Dracula was intended to hang on a door during Halloween time, but I attached him to a pillowcase. I added four squares of material and cut a slit above each one. Next, I added Velcro dots to each square. For this activity, I added numerals to each of the dots. Then, the students used a collection of small toys (think McDonald's Happy Meals) to sort by counting the syllables with Count Dracula. The kids then dropped each toy into the correct slit. The numerals can be easily changed to letters for beginning sounds or to pictures for matching phonemes.

Although these sand castles are found in the toy section, I still consider them a seasonal item since we tend to see them during the summer shopping season. I'm always looking for sets of three. (This sand castle has three towers, for instance.) By adding a set of letters with Velcro dots, kids can build sandcastle words with the pattern of consonant/vowel/consonant.

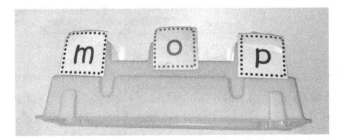

These little cars found in the toy section provide opportunities for kids to segment phonemes by racing the cars into the parking spaces for each phoneme. These are great for working with small groups during your instructional group time. Instead of reviewing 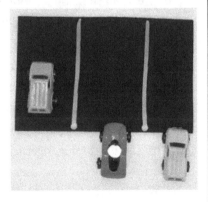 segmenting with your students by filling out a worksheet or placing magnetic letters on a board, say a word like "cat" and let your students drive the cars into place as they say "/c/, /a/, /t/."

These are just a few activity creations from my many great finds from dollar stores. The possibilities of items you can discover are limitless, if you use your imagination. Dollar store shopping provides an opportunity to create environments and experiences that captivate and motivate our kids in a way that stretches the dollar. But it can also inspire you! As you walk the aisles and think of new ways to teach difficult concepts, you hone your craft. You think of ways to reach that child that has not been motivated with traditional teaching strategies. You become excited yourself. You start to see the fun part of teaching again. Creating and learning isn't just for the kids. It's for us, too! Happy shopping!

—Kim Adsit, kindergals.blogspot.com

Great minds think alike, right? It would seem that way since both Kim and I agree that taking a friend with you to the dollar store is better than going alone. We aren't the only teachers who feel this way, and I was beyond excited when I was asked to accompany a group of pre-K teachers on a shopping trip as part of their back-to-school teacher training days! I had been booked by a school in New Orleans to do a full-day workshop on play-based learning and was geared up to work with some amazing educators who were eager to include more hands-on activities in their classrooms.

A few days before the visit, I got a call from the assistant principal requesting that we spend part of the day carpooling to a local dollar store and working together with the teachers to purchase items like the ones they had seen in my YouTube series. I agreed and, let me tell you, it was a blast! Picture eighteen teachers filing into a store, browsing every single aisle, loading baskets and carts, and leaving together. Let's just say we turned quite a few heads that day, not to mention we cleaned out entire sections of items to create some incredible games! Though I was having a great time helping these teachers, my favorite part was simply watching their imaginations and creativity pour into this project. They came up with ideas for games that I had never thought of before, using items I had never even considered picking up on my previous visits.

I encourage you to visit a local dollar store with no specific items in mind. Grab a shopping cart or basket and start strolling around the aisles. Use your imagination, think about your students, and start loading your cart with items that will engage and excite. If you are able, take a teacher friend or an entire group of teachers along with you to maximize the fun and your results!

Conclusion
JUST THE BEGINNING

"**WE COULD NEVER** have loved the Earth so well if we had had no childhood in it." These are the words of author George Eliot. They are the perfect way to introduce our chapter on playing outside and learning while enjoying our beautiful planet. In fact, I don't believe I can write a thorough book on play without discussing playing outside. Unfortunately, children don't experience outside play nearly enough anymore. I'll be honest by saying that I probably don't get outside as much as I should with my own kids because of that overscheduled, overwhelming lifestyle Dr. Jean mentions in the foreword. That said, our family tries to spend as much time outdoors as we possibly can during the warmer months in Illinois.

Thinking about this subject really made me reflect on whether I had allowed enough outside play with my students. And if I'm struggling to find time to play outside with my own kids, then the parents of my students had probably been struggling, too, right? And what about the parents who leave for work before it's light outside and get home after dark? School might be the only time some students get to go outside and play. I'm not talking about free play at recess, which I do believe is a very important part of the day. I'm talking about structured, purposeful play—play based on the same philosophies shared throughout this book, only outside.

PLAY BEYOND THE CLASSROOM

Trisha is nothing short of a genius when it comes to thinking of ways for her students to learn outside the four walls of her classroom. Whether it be games that take her students around the school or lessons taught from the playground, I have learned so much from her in this area. I'm going to start with an idea that my wife Trisha tried with her students that brought amazing results.

GAGA BALL

Ever heard of gaga ball? I hadn't until my kids came home from school one day and couldn't wait to tell me about a new structure on their school playground. Gaga ball is played inside an eight-sided pit by any number of players. The rules are simple.

1. Everyone starts with one hand on the side of the pit.
2. One player starts the game by hitting the ball across the pit.
3. Players can use only their hands to hit or deflect the ball.
4. No player can hit the ball twice in a row.
5. If the ball hits a player at the waist or below, that player is out.
6. Play continues until only one player remains in the pit.

Family gaga ball is the best! (Trisha was already out.)

It really is a pretty fun game to play, and it's a great workout as well. Every day for the first few weeks after the pit had been installed at school, both my kids would come home talking about the latest gaga ball match at recess that day. They weren't the only ones going on and on about this game though. Trisha also had story after story about how thrilled her students were with the game and how they wouldn't stop talking about gaga ball in the classroom.

This is where her genius idea to adapt this game comes in. Her class was working on graphing during their math block, and the weather outside at this time just happened to be perfect. Trisha is so good at making last-minute decisions in the classroom to teach her content in a way that relates to her students. Why not take the class outside to do a meaningful and fun graphing activity? She announced to the class that they were going to do math outside that day, and cheers erupted from every single student. What she thought was excitement was quickly put to shame when she then told them they were going out to play gaga ball for math. She heard no cheers this time, just screams!

121

She took her class outside to play two games of gaga ball. Though they were playing the game following the regular rules, students had to remember the number of times they hit the ball in each game. Obviously, this number was very different from student to student, depending on what direction the ball was hit and how quickly each kid got knocked out. When the class finished playing both games, they completed a line plot recording the data of how many times each student in the class hit the ball. The engagement was there, the activity was there, the enjoyment was without a doubt there, and her students mastered line plotting faster than ever before!

Gaga ball + line plots = smiles.

If you want to try this fun game at home sometime, you should know that a gaga ball pit isn't necessary. Our kids have introduced us to trampoline gaga ball, and we have a blast playing it in the backyard. But don't limit this type of activity to gaga ball. Trisha could have done the same type of line plotting lesson by letting the kids shoot baskets, kick soccer goals, or count hits in a game of dodgeball. Try to do something similar with a lesson that has your students tracking and recording data of some type. Use their interests as the engagement factor, then add some activity to your lesson. You, too, will see more enjoyment on the faces of your students!

PLAYGROUND LESSONS

Trisha's idea is the perfect bit of proof that when you don't let the pages of your curriculum or the walls of your classroom limit you, you can turn any standards-driven task into a fun and engaging activity. No gaga ball pit, no problem! Look closely around the playground at your school. Hopefully it's full of equipment for your students to run, climb, and swing on. Now take a closer look.

How many rungs are on the ladders?

How many links make up the chains holding up the swings?

Are there more or fewer rungs on the monkey bars than the ladder leading up to them? What are the angles of the slides, and are they the same or different from each other? What shapes do you see when you look closely at the different pieces of equipment? Can you find any letters hidden in the playground scene?

One of my good friends and coworkers answered that last question with pictures when his daughter was in my kindergarten class. As an end-of-the-year gift, he and his daughter gave me this very creative project to decorate my classroom! How cool is that? It's a priceless piece that I will treasure forever, and it is proof that even the smallest of learning targets can be reached in creative ways if you think outside of the norm. Thanks to the Z family for this unique gift!

Love, Payton 2014/15

The playground at your school is the perfect place to go when you reach the measurement unit in the scope and sequence of your math curriculum. Collect some tape measures, rulers, and yardsticks, and head outside! There are so many different things to measure on a playground, and because of the 3D aspect of it, your students can find objects with length, width, depth, radius, and circumference just by exploring.

On the playground is also where we can put the stigma of worksheets to rest. It is a well-known fact that I am not a fan of workbooks and worksheets. While I understand that children need to learn to put pencil to paper to solve problems and answer questions, I believe there's always an opportunity to do more. Worksheets torn from workbooks typically limit creativity, and they don't allow children to use their individual thought processes to solve problems. After your students have a basic understanding of the topic and have learned the appropriate terminology, such as with the measurement activity, you can take the skills from a typical worksheet and turn your children loose. So instead of everyone measuring the length of the same pencils and crayons and markers, your students will be finding their own items to measure, determining what dimensions they will measure, and figuring out how best to measure the items they choose. The best part is that all of this great work is going on while your students are running around in the fresh air doing what they do best—being kids!

ENVIRONMENTALLY FRIENDLY FRIENDS

One of my favorite aspects of the Next Generation Science Standards is the focus on teaching children to recognize and execute ways to take care of the world around them. In the NGSS domain of Earth and Space Science, you'll find the following standard: Communicate solutions that will reduce the impact of humans on the land, water, air, and/or other living things in the local environment.

Textbooks, books, and videos can all help children understand the importance of taking care of the environment. Numerous online resources drive home the importance of such topics as well. But remember, this chapter is all about getting outside the classroom. So instead of simply listening or reading about what we can do, get outside and do it!

Every year around Earth Day, my students and I would put everything we've learned to good use. We'd don rubber gloves and safety goggles, grab some garbage bags, and hit the land around our school running! We would pick up garbage and recyclable materials and sort them into separate bags. We cleaned up the playground, the soccer fields, and the bushes around the school building. When we were finished, we'd talk about all the ways we actually helped the environment by doing what we did. My students were engaged, they were active, and they were very much enjoying themselves. They were playing while happily taking care of the world around them!

NOT JUST LEARNING, WANTING TO LEARN

I know I've used quite a few quotes from inspiring educators through the chapters we've covered so far, but I don't believe I can end the book without quoting who I believe is one of the most influential people ever to have taken a stand on the topic of play, Mr. Rogers. Fred Rogers never spoke truer words: "Play is often talked about as if it were a relief from serious learning. But for children, play is serious learning. Play is really the work of childhood."

I absolutely love this quote from Mr. Rogers, who I believe was one of the most important advocates and strongest voices for early education. I think it is the perfect quote for summing up everything I've tried to get across in this book. Whenever I needed to justify the existence of play in my classroom, Mr. Rogers's quote was the only answer I needed. Kids are never *just* playing!

Now, take that mindset and couple it with all your lessons and all the activities you have in your classroom. When you do, I know you'll find great success in bringing your curriculum to life like never before. Your students will love playing new games, creating with new manipulatives, and learning in new ways. But never forget that those items are just tools of our trade. When it comes to the real substance of the classroom, you are the most important piece of the puzzle!

It is my sincere hope that you're already using a lot of these types of activities with your students, but I also hope that my sharing these ideas has reignited something in your mind and heart. While I've mentioned all along that you can create an environment of play-based learning very easily, it may also be a bit overwhelming with all the ideas and activities my friends and I have shared. My advice to you is the same I give when I speak to college students or first-year teachers. I strongly encourage you to take it slow, and don't try to do too much too fast. You need to make sure you have your expectations in place and positive relationships built among your students before any of these concepts will take hold in your classroom. Without the proper environment to run a play-driven learning space, it will never thrive. You'll be spending valuable time correcting student behaviors and micromanaging your groups, and your time spent on individualized work with students and addressing their needs will be stretched.

Once you have a healthy learning environment in place, I challenge you to start slowly adding a play-based approach into your routine. Focus on one lesson to start. Yes, just one. Take a lesson you feel extremely comfortable teaching, one that involves standards you know inside and out. Remember, familiarity is key. Maybe try to pick a lesson that lacks the key components of the definition of play in one way or another. Try a lesson that your students are engaged in but that lacks activity and enjoyment. Now think of ways you can increase the activity and enjoyment for your students by focusing on *how* you're going to teach the *what*. Repeat this process with a different lesson each week, and you'll soon have an entire arsenal of lessons that you can use to implement a full-blown play-based learning approach in your classroom that will have your students excited to come to school to learn each day!

Excitement. Maybe that's another word that should be added to the dictionary's definition of play. Think back to your time in the classroom as a child. What made you most excited? I can almost guarantee that most readers are answering that question with some favorite toys, games, or areas of their classrooms. But the majority of answers will also most likely include the same thing that I remember excited me: my teachers! I remember some fun things that I did as a child throughout elementary school. I remember field trips my teachers took us on, some toys and games my teachers introduced us to, and some really amazing units my teachers incorporated into the curriculum. But none of those things would be at the forefront of my memories, or would have even been possible, without my amazing teachers.

Teachers. That's what I remember most. Take away all the stuff, the games, the units, the field trips. All of it, gone! I would still be able to recall some hugely significant things and remember that my excitement for school was because of my teachers. When they're asked the same question, I hope this is what your students will say: "My favorite part of school was [insert your name here]!" Be the teacher that gets your students excited to walk through the door every day with smiles on their faces. The kids are going to learn all the things we need them to at some point in their educational career. It is our responsibility to create an environment that fosters engagement, enjoyment, and activity so every single child that walks through our door *wants* to keep coming back and *wants* to learn.

Good luck! The cards are in your hands now!

REFERENCES

PRINT REFERENCES

Armstrong, Thomas. 2011. "Early Childhood Education
Programs: Play." Association for Supervision and Curriculum
Development. ascd.org/publications/books/106044 /chapters/
Early-Childhood-Education-Programs.

Brown, Stuart. 2009. *Play: How It Shapes the Brain*. New York:
Penguin Books.

Dewar, Gwen. 2014. "The Cognitive Benefits of Play: Effects on
the Learning Brain." Parenting Science. parentingscience.com/
benefits-of-play

Elkind, David. 2007. *The Power of Play: How Spontaneous,
Imaginative Activities Lead to Happier, Healthier Children*.
Cambridge, MA: Da Capo Press.

Ginsburg, Kenneth. 2007. "The Importance of Play in Promoting Healthy Child Development and Maintaining Strong Pare-Child Bonds." *Pediatrics* 119 (1): 182–191.

Hannaford, Carla. 2005. *Smart Moves: Why Learning Is Not All in Your Head.* Salt Lake City, UT: Great River Books.

Jensen, Eric. 2005. *Teaching with the Brain in Mind.* Alexandria, VA: ASCD.

Louv, Richard. 2005. *Last Child in the Woods.* Chapel Hill, NC: Algonquin Books.

Miller, Edward, and Joan Almon. 2009. *Crisis in the Kindergarten: Why Children Need to Play in School.* College Park, MD: Alliance for Childhood.

Ratey, John. 2008. *Spark: The Revolutionary New Science of Exercise and the Brain.* New York: Little Brown and Company.

WEB RESOURCES

allianceforchildhood.org/sites/allianceforchildhood.org/files/file/kindergarten_report.pdf

naeyc.org

nifplay.org

ipausa.org (American Association for the Child's Right to Play)

ACKNOWLEDGEMENTS

I need to first start by thanking my family. When it comes to inspiration for anything I do, Trisha and our kids have always been behind me 100 percent. Trisha, thank you for believing in me and supporting my decisions, no matter how crazy they are sometimes. Olivia and Landon, thank you for always being my biggest fans! I love the three of you more than you'll ever know.

Thank you to my mom and dad. It's no secret that I haven't always made parenting easy on the two of you, but you never gave up on loving, supporting, and encouraging me. I hope someday I can repay you for everything you've done for me and my family.

Thank you to my mother-in-law, Gloria for your continued support of every project I start! I could never thank you enough for all the ways you have helped our family.

To Jodie, Shannon, Lily, Dean, Maurey, Michael, Jon, Jen, Scott, Nanny Lois, and Grandma Caroll. Family means everything to me, and none of my success would be possible without the support of you all.

For always being willing to share your brilliant ideas and suggestions with me, and with educators around the world, thank you to Dr. Jean Feldman, Kim Adsit, Jamie Hubbard, Kurt Schwengel, Adam Dovico, Dr. Lori Elliott, Deedee Wills, Hilary Statum, Kim Bearden, Jessica Travis, Kim Jordano, Shari Smith Sloane, and so many more.

A special thank you to my friends Emily Hawkins, Kymra Kurinskas, everyone at SDE, Ryan Nevius, Channon Morris, Melinda Cook McDonald, Kristen Sloan, everyone at ESGI, Dr. Craig Vivian, Melinda Grimm, Russ Farmer, Taryn Trotter, Shannon Hamm, Joe Zweeres, Liz Peterson, Kathy Perry, and everyone at Saratoga Elementary School, who have all believed in and supported my ideas as a teacher and a presenter.

Thank you all the parents and families who trusted me with their children in my classroom. I wouldn't be the teacher I am today if it weren't for the lessons I learned from every child that walked through the door of room 106.

To the hundreds, thousands, and millions of other educators who are working endlessly, day in and day out, to create amazing environments for young learners, THANK YOU for all you do!

Last, but not least, thank you to Dave and Shelley Burgess for taking a chance on me and believing in this idea of mine. When folks of their expertise take an interest in play-driven learning, I get really excited for the future of schools! Their passion for education is admirable, and their support of teachers is second to none.

ABOUT THE AUTHOR

ADAM PETERSON is an award-winning educator from Illinois and a nationally recognized speaker. After spending more than a decade as a kindergarten teacher, Adam now uses his knowledge and talents to inspire, educate, and motivate other teachers to create classrooms that encourage creativity, play, and hands-on learning. When he's not working with teachers on location, Adam spends his time at home creating YouTube videos for teachers, co-hosting the popular podcast *The Classroom Collaborative* with Deedee Wills, and writing any chance he gets. Adam's most recent accomplishment was being a featured speaker at the event TEDxNormal 2019, where he shared his message of making the world a brighter place through his Be the Yellow talk and his #betheyellow campaign! Being a believer that family comes first, Adam spends every free second he has with his beautiful wife, Trisha, and their two amazing children.

For more information on where to see Adam speak, or to book him for your own school, visit his website adampetersoneducation.com. You can keep up with him on Instagram (@teacherslearn2) and Twitter (@teacherslearn2). Visit makesomeonesdayyellow.com to learn how to get this inspiring event started at your own school!

SPEAKING TOPICS

KEYNOTE: BE THE YELLOW:
SIX STEPS TO A KINDER WORLD

AUDIENCE: ALL GRADES, ADMIN, BUSINESS, ETC.

In this inspiring keynote address, Adam shares his six-step process for making the world a brighter and kinder place, all by focusing on something as simple as a color. Adam shares personal experiences and stories that led him to write a children's book and start a movement that has reached students and teachers in over thirty states and eight countries around the world. Whether you're a teacher, parent, businessperson, or CEO, you are sure to be motivated, inspired, and moved to do all you can to spread the YELLOW when you leave this session.

KEYNOTE:
EVERY DAY IS THE B.E.S.T. DAY EVER

AUDIENCE: ALL GRADES, ADMIN

Turn every day in your classroom into the most positive experience possible! This motivational message is full of ideas to easily implement Adam's B.E.S.T. Day Ever routine into your own classroom. From building relationships to going above and beyond the expectations, Adam's tips and tricks will have you laughing, learning, and ready to head back to your classroom!

TEACH. PLAY. LEARN!

AUDIENCE: PREK-3 TEACHERS, ADMIN

Ever feel like you're bogged down with curriculum, standards, and new manuals? Well, never fear, Adam is here! Using tried and true methods, Adam will have you laughing, moving, playing, and learning as you explore ways to make your standards more fun than ever before. With simple tweaks and classroom hacks to board games, card games, and more, you can have your students of any age learning through play in so many ways!

MODEL, MOTIVATE, WRITE, REPEAT!

AUDIENCE: PREK-2 TEACHERS, ADMIN

From tried and true techniques to publishing books with your students, this session has it all! Adam uses personal classroom experiences to give you all the help you need to create engaging lessons that will excite your students about writing. Through easy modeling, engaging motivational activities, and simple and creative books, your students will be ready to write like never before!

NEXT GENERATION STUDENT SCIENTISTS

AUDIENCE: PREK-2 TEACHERS, ADMIN

Learning the science standards has never been more fun than this. With a few surprises and exciting twists to your curriculum, Adam will show you ways to make science come alive in your classroom. This hands-on session will have you and your staff working together to solve problems in ways that can be adapted for even the youngest of learners!

WHOA! WHAT HAPPENED TO OUR CLASSROOM?!?!

AUDIENCE: ALL GRADES, ADMIN

What?! Wow! Awesome! Those are words every teacher loves to hear, right? Adam's love of teaching, combined with his creativity, had his students saying this quite often. Whether it's for a class party, book review, or to boost engagement, Adam's room flips are sure to excite even the most reluctant learners. Take a trip through a wild forest, go on a Pokémon hunt, explore a bat cave, and more in this fun learning experience.

MORE TEACHING METHODS & MATERIALS

All 4s and 5s by Andrew Sharos

Boredom Busters by Katie Powell

The Classroom Chef by John Stevens and Matt Vaudrey

The Collaborative Classroom by Trevor Muir

Copyrighteous by Diana Gill

Ditch That Homework by Matt Miller and Alice Keeler

Ditch That Textbook by Matt Miller

Don't Ditch That Tech by Matt Miller, Nate Ridgway, and Angelia Ridgway

EDrenaline Rush by John Meehan

Educated by Design by Michael Cohen, The Tech Rabbi

The EduProtocol Field Guide by Marlena Hebern and Jon Corippo

The EduProtocol Field Guide: Book 2 by Marlena Hebern and Jon Corippo

Instant Relevance by Denis Sheeran

LAUNCH by John Spencer and A.J. Juliani

Make Learning MAGICAL by Tisha Richmond

Pure Genius by Don Wettrick

The Revolution by Darren Ellwein and Derek McCoy

Shift This! by Joy Kirr

Skyrocket Your Teacher Coaching by Michael Cary Sonbert

Spark Learning by Ramsey Musallam

Sparks in the Dark by Travis Crowder and Todd Nesloney

Table Talk Math by John Stevens

The Wild Card by Hope and Wade King

The Writing on the Classroom Wall by Steve Wyborney

LIKE A PIRATE™ SERIES

Teach Like a PIRATE by Dave Burgess

eXPlore Like a Pirate by Michael Matera

Learn Like a Pirate by Paul Solarz

Play Like a Pirate by Quinn Rollins

Run Like a Pirate by Adam Welcome

LEAD LIKE A PIRATE™ SERIES

Lead Like a PIRATE by Shelley Burgess and Beth Houf

Balance Like a Pirate by Jessica Cabeen, Jessica Johnson, and
     Sarah Johnson

Lead beyond Your Title by Nili Bartley

Lead with Appreciation by Amber Teamann and Melinda Miller

Lead with Culture by Jay Billy

Lead with Instructional Rounds by Vicki Wilson

Lead with Literacy by Mandy Ellis

LEADERSHIP & SCHOOL CULTURE

Culturize by Jimmy Casas

Escaping the School Leader's Dunk Tank by Rebecca Coda and Rick Jetter

From Teacher to Leader by Starr Sackstein

The Innovator's Mindset by George Couros

It's OK to Say "They" by Christy Whittlesey

Kids Deserve It! by Todd Nesloney and Adam Welcome

Live Your Excellence by Jimmy Casas

Let Them Speak by Rebecca Coda and Rick Jetter

The Limitless School by Abe Hege and Adam Dovico

Next-Level Teaching by Jonathan Alsheimer

The Pepper Effect by Sean Gaillard

The Principled Principal by Jeffrey Zoul and Anthony McConnell

Relentless by Hamish Brewer

The Secret Solution by Todd Whitaker, Sam Miller, and Ryan Donlan

Start. Right. Now. by Todd Whitaker, Jeffrey Zoul, and Jimmy Casas

Stop. Right. Now. by Jimmy Casas and Jeffrey Zoul

They Call Me "Mr. De" by Frank DeAngelis

Unmapped Potential by Julie Hasson and Missy Lennard

Word Shift by Joy Kirr

Your School Rocks by Ryan McLane and Eric Lowe

TECHNOLOGY & TOOLS

50 Things You Can Do with Google Classroom by Alice Keeler and Libbi Miller

50 Things to Go Further with Google Classroom by Alice Keeler and Libbi Miller

140 Twitter Tips for Educators by Brad Currie, Billy Krakower, and Scott Rocco

Block Breaker by Brian Aspinall

Code Breaker by Brian Aspinall

Google Apps for Littles by Christine Pinto and Alice Keeler

Master the Media by Julie Smith

Reality Bytes by Christine Lion-Bailey, Jesse Lubinsky, Micah Shippee, PhD

Shake Up Learning by Kasey Bell

Social LEADia by Jennifer Casa-Todd

Teaching Math with Google Apps by Alice Keeler and Diana Herrington

Teachingland by Amanda Fox and Mary Ellen Weeks

INSPIRATION, PROFESSIONAL GROWTH & PERSONAL DEVELOPMENT

Be REAL by Tara Martin

Be the One for Kids by Ryan Sheehy

The Coach ADVenture by Amy Illingworth

Creatively Productive by Lisa Johnson

Educational Eye Exam by Alicia Ray

The EduNinja Mindset by Jennifer Burdis

Empower Our Girls by Lynmara Colón and Adam Welcome

Finding Lifelines by Andrew Grieve and Andrew Sharos

The Four O'Clock Faculty by Rich Czyz

How Much Water Do We Have? by Pete and Kris Nunweiler

P Is for Pirate by Dave and Shelley Burgess

A Passion for Kindness by Tamara Letter

The Path to Serendipity by Allyson Apsey

Sanctuaries by Dan Tricarico

The SECRET SAUCE by Rich Czyz

Shattering the Perfect Teacher Myth by Aaron Hogan

Stories from Webb by Todd Nesloney

Talk to Me by Kim Bearden

Teach Better by Chad Ostrowski, Tiffany Ott, Rae Hughart, and
     Jeff Gargas

Teach Me, Teacher by Jacob Chastain

TeamMakers by Laura Robb and Evan Robb

Through the Lens of Serendipity by Allyson Apsey

The Zen Teacher by Dan Tricarico

CHILDREN'S BOOKS

Beyond Us by Aaron Polansky

Cannonball In by Tara Martin

Dolphins in Trees by Aaron Polansky

I Want to Be a Lot by Ashley Savage

The Princes of Serendip by Allyson Apsey

The Wild Card Kids by Hope and Wade King

Zom-Be a Design Thinker by Amanda Fox

CPSIA information can be obtained
at www.ICGtesting.com
Printed in the USA
LVHW021341100521
686964LV00014B/1304